THE CRIME BUFF'S GUIDE TO THE OUTLAW ROCKIES

RON FRANSCELL

Guilford, Connecticut

To Bill Vandeventer,
who has always had room

Guilford, Connectic

Copyright © 2011 by Ron Franscell

All photos by Ron Franscell unless otherwise noted.
Text design: Sheryl P. Kober
Layout: Justin Marciano
Project editor: Meredith Dias
Maps by Melissa Baker © Morris Book Publishing, LLC

Library of Congress Cataloging-in-Publication Data is available on file.

ISBN 978-0-7627-7163-9

Printed in the United States of America
10 9 8 7 6 5 4 3 2

CONTENTS

Introduction **vii**

How to Use This Book **ix**

A Note about GPS Accuracy **ix**

Chapter 1: Denver Metro Area **1**

Chapter 2: Colorado Front Range **41**

Chapter 3: Colorado Western Slope **92**

Chapter 4: Butch Cassidy, the Sundance Kid,

and the Wild Bunch **120**

Chapter 5: Wyoming **143**

Acknowledgments **223**

Index **225**

About the Author **230**

COVER PHOTOS KEY

(All cover photos by the author.)

1. Madam Mattie Silks's bordello at 2009 Market Street is a historic Denver landmark today. (Fairmount Cemetery, page 28)

2. Old-timers once recalled "Uncle" Butch Cassidy pitching silver dollars to them from the door of the Miner's Exchange Saloon in South Pass City. (Miner's Exchange Saloon, page 133)

3. Towering twelve stories above the North Platte, this bridge was the site of the rape of one young Casper girl and murder of another in 1973, a crime that still haunts the city. (Fremont Canyon Bridge Murder, page 153)

4. A visitor center on the site of the Ludlow camp near Trinidad memorializes the twenty-five dead—mostly women and children—in the strike-breaking attack. (Ludlow Massacre, page 86)

5. Gay college student Matthew Shepard was brutally beaten by two local thugs and left to die on this buckrail fence in 1998. (Matthew Shepard Murder, page 187)

6. Nobody knows exactly where Kid Curry was buried in Linwood Cemetery after his suicide, but a marker exists anyway. (Harvey "Kid Curry" Logan's Grave, page 136)

7. Tyrannical father Richard Jahnke was killed by his son in front of the garage at this house in 1982. (Richard Jahnke Murder, page 166)

8. Former teacher Fred Lundy, who lived in this mountain cabin, helped the Griffith sisters build a cabin nearby—and might have killed them too. (Emily Griffith Murder, page 77)

9. Gaetano's, a restaurant that advertises "Italian to die for," was the headquarters for Denver's mob underworld for decades. (Denver's Brother Hoods, page 38)

GHOSTS OF THE WILDEST WEST: AN INTRODUCTION

Ask yourself this question: What made the Wild West *wild*?

Was it an untamed landscape that was as unforgiving as it was magnificent? Was it a primitive sense that no amount of money or breeding could save you from its dangers? Or could it have been the unchecked lawlessness that prevailed for decades—and still exists in its most remote corners?

Or maybe it was all those things.

Place matters, even in crime. I grew up in Wyoming, and I understand how it's possible to drive a long, straight road for hours without ever seeing another human. I know how lofty philosophies about law and justice dissolve in remote places where cries for help will go unheard. I have spent moonless nights beneath skies so inky black that you cannot see your fingers in front of your face—perfect for those who would hide their faces and deeds.

Being there is not just a good way to understand history, but in some places, it helps you grasp the desperation and loneliness of the people who were there before you, especially in places where our imagination, myth, and history entangle. Places where the past exists just beneath the surface of the present.

This book will take you to the lonely swale where a Colorado brewing magnate died unexpectedly on a crisp morning. It will let you stand where a sixteen-year-old boy ended one of Wyoming's deadliest killing sprees with a single shot. It will point the way to spots where infamous crime figures—Bat Masterson, Charlie Starkweather, Doc Holliday, Al Capone, Butch Cassidy, and Ted Bundy, among others—once stood. It will take you to the many places in our Wildest West where ordinarily law-abiding people finally grew frustrated with the pace of justice and took the law into their own hands.

Let this book be your window. Our appreciation of history begins in the places where it happened. And now the magic of the Global Positioning System (GPS) allows you to stand in a precise historic spot, as best as our modern technology and imaginations can muster. We have made every attempt to put you literally within inches of the past.

This is certainly no ordinary guidebook. You won't find many suggestions for places to sleep or eat, although you might often find such spots by chasing these ghosts. Rather, consider this a history book that tells you exactly where to stand to see the past and present—and maybe a bit of the future.

The Wild West is many things, not the least of which is a wild history of crime, punishment, survival, and redemption.

History is how we know, how we learn. And being there makes all the difference.

—RON FRANSCELL

HOW TO USE THIS BOOK

The entries in this book are divided into five chapters: four geographic regions (Metro Denver, Colorado's Front Range and Western Slope, and Wyoming) and one segment about the famous outlaw Butch Cassidy and his Wild Bunch. Each entry has physical and GPS directions that will let you stand in the footsteps of history—not in the general vicinity, but literally on a spot relevant to one of Colorado's or Wyoming's most notable and fascinating crimes or outlaw-related figures.

Crimes big and small have been committed every single day since mankind began to distinguish right from wrong. This book cannot begin to aggregate every injustice, every crime, every inhumanity ever visited upon Colorado and Wyoming, although even the smallest crime certainly affects victims, survivors, and communities as much as the most celebrated crimes in our history. And in some cases here, I have chosen only a few representative sites. So please don't be offended if you feel I've overlooked a crime or site you believe should have been included.

A word of warning: Many of these sites are on private property. Always seek permission before venturing onto private land. Do not trespass. It's rude, it's illegal, and this is still the Wild West, where everybody owns a gun.

I made every effort to be precise in my facts and directions, but being human, I am bound to have erred here and there. If you believe I should include a certain crime in future editions—or if you see an error that should be corrected—please send me a note at Ron Franscell/ OUTLAW ROCKIES, c/o Globe Pequot Press, 246 Goose Lane, P.O. Box 480, Guilford, CT 06437; or e-mail editorial@globepequot.com.

A NOTE ABOUT GPS ACCURACY

GPS readings are affected by many things, including satellite positions, noise in the radio signal, weather, natural barriers to the signal, and variations between devices. Noise—static, interference, or competing frequencies—can cause errors up to thirty feet. Clouds, bad weather, mountains, or buildings can also skew readings up to one hundred feet.

While I've tried to make every GPS coordinate in *The Crime Buff's Guide to the Outlaw Rockies* as precise as possible, I can't be sure you'll visit under the same conditions or with the same kind of equipment. The best possible way to get an accurate reading is to be sure the satellites and your receiver have a clear view of each other, with no clouds, trees, or other interference. If your device doesn't bring you to the right spot, look around. It's likely within a few paces.

1

DENVER METRO AREA

CHUCK E. CHEESE MASS MURDER
Aurora

The building that once housed the Chuck E. Cheese restaurant is in a strip mall at 12293 East Iliff Ave., Suite A. GPS 39.675207, -104.844887

Less than two weeks before Christmas in 1994, Nathan Dunlap—an angry kitchen worker who'd been fired a week before—slipped into the Chuck E. Cheese pizzeria just after closing. In a murderous rage, he shot five former coworkers (three of them teenagers) with a small-caliber, semiautomatic handgun. Four of them died on the spot, but despite being shot in the jaw, a fifth escaped to a nearby apartment building where he called police.

Dunlap, twenty, escaped and was hidden by his girlfriend until he was arrested the next day. He was convicted in the mass murder two years later and given four death sentences, one for each of the victims gunned down at the pizza parlor. He remains on Colorado's death row.

DEATH ROW'S LUCKIEST MAN
Aurora

Eastlawn Memorial Gardens is at 19600 Smith Rd. The grave is at GPS 39.75053, -104.75159.

Three times, convicted killer Sylvester Lee Garrison (1932–2005) ate his last meal—always fried chicken, stewed onions, french fries and "real" coffee—before eleventh-hour stays saved his life. In eleven years on death row, he shook the hands of five condemned men who never came back from the gas chamber. He himself had fourteen

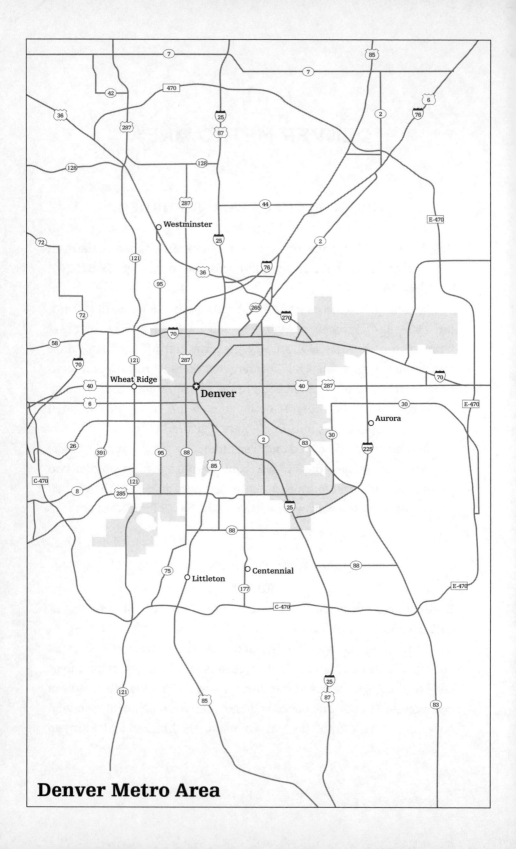

Denver Metro Area

different execution dates for the 1958 pistol-whipping murder of an elderly man—but all came and went as Garrison, who always said he didn't do it, survived.

When the U.S. Supreme Court abolished the death penalty in 1972, Garrison's sentence was commuted to life. Despite his murder conviction, he was paroled in 1978 and became a city maintenance worker and beloved family patriarch, still maintaining his innocence.

He grew philosophical about what he'd seen while awaiting his own death.

"You could see all the weak parts of people, the child in them," he told a newspaperman in 1989. "I seen some of them fantasize and never come back."

"How many times can you die?" he once asked. Well, Garrison escaped death row and became a kind of poster boy for capital punishment opponents, but he couldn't escape death. He died of a brain tumor in 2005, just a week shy of his seventy-third birthday.

FALLEN OFFICERS MEMORIAL
Aurora
This memorial is in the City of Aurora's government complex at 15151 East Alameda Parkway, or GPS 39.71154, -104.81341.

This site is among the most ambitious and contemplative memorials ever created to honor police officers who have died in the line of duty. Sculpture and a somber wall of memory pay tribute to the local lawmen and women.

VICTIM ALIE BERRELEZ'S GRAVE
Centennial
Chapel Hill Memorial Gardens is at 6601 S. Colorado Blvd., or GPS 39.59981, -104.94614.

Aleszandra "Alie" Berrelez (1988–1993) was only five years old when she was abducted from the yard of her family's Englewood

*The city of Aurora pays tribute to
fallen officers at an elaborate, touching
memorial.*

apartment building on May 18, 1993. Four days later, a police bloodhound named Yogi led his handler over more than fourteen miles
of rugged terrain to her smothered body, which had been stuffed
in a khaki duffel bag and dumped down a ravine near Deer Creek
Mountain Park.

Yogi tracked the killer's scent back to an empty apartment in
Alie's apartment building, but to date, the case is unsolved. Police
believe Alie's killer either lived in the apartment complex or had
visited someone there.

The slain girl's grandparents established the Alie Foundation, which buys bloodhounds for police agencies throughout the United States. Since then, the nonprofit foundation has placed more than three hundred bloodhounds in forty-five states.

Yogi died of cancer in 1998. He is buried with twenty other police dogs at the Aurora Police Shooting Range at the Spring Hill Golf Course, 810 Telluride St., or GPS 39.72957, -104.77373.

You can learn more about the Alie Foundation at its website: www.alie.org.

- Columbine High School massacre victims **Corey DePooter, Rachel Scott,** and teacher **Dave Sanders** are all buried in Chapel Hill Memorial Gardens in Centennial. DePooter and Scott are buried side by side in the Columbine Memorial at GPS 39.60139, -104.94952. Sanders is buried in Section 394, or GPS 39.60094, -104.94704.

See also Fallen Officers Memorial.

A police bloodhound, Yogi found Alie Berrelez's body more than nine miles from where she disappeared.

ALAN BERG'S MURDER SCENE
Denver

Berg's former townhouse is at 1445 Adams St., or GPS 39.73931, -104.94850. This is private property.

Talk-radio host Alan Berg (1934–1984) had a knack for riling people up. Using the thirty-eight-state broadcasting reach of Denver's KOA radio station, the Chicago-born liberal provoked and enraged listeners on topics like oral sex, bigotry, Christianity, gun control, and neo-Nazis. Abrasive and irreverent, he took no prisoners: He often insulted any callers who dared disagree with him, including the Colorado secretary of state. Berg was so potent, he was profiled by *60 Minutes'* Morley Safer. He proudly called himself "the man Denver loves to hate." In short, he was the irascible model for later talk-radio icons like Rush Limbaugh.

Naturally, Berg picked up enemies. Among them were members of a growing white supremacist group called The Order. The devoutly anti-Semitic organization kept a "hate list" of people it deemed to be threats to the white race—people it believed should be assassinated. Among them were Henry Kissinger, Norman Lear, David Rockefeller—and Alan Berg.

On June 18, 1984, Berg was shot thirteen times with an assault rifle in the driveway of his town home by members of The Order. The hit was financed with money stolen in bank robberies.

Two Order members—shooter Bruce Pierce and getaway driver David Lane—were convicted in 1987, not for killing Berg but for violating his civil rights. Pierce is still serving his 252-year sentence in a Pennsylvania federal prison; Lane died in an Indiana prison in 2007 of an epileptic seizure. Other Order members were suspected of playing roles in the murder but never convicted.

Berg's story was told in Stephen Singular's 1987 book *Talked to Death* and fictionalized by director Oliver Stone in his 1988 movie *Talk Radio*.

DENVER MINT ROBBERY
Denver
The Mint is at 320 West Colfax Ave., or GPS 39.7399, -104.992336.

A famous bank robber once said he robbed banks because that's where the money is. But on a frigid morning in December 1922, a gang of thieves went directly to where the money is *made*—the Denver Mint—to hijack an armored car containing $200,000 in $5 bills. In ninety seconds outside the Mint's front door on West Colfax Avenue, five robbers drove up in a black Buick, killed a guard, and grabbed the money. In the ensuing gunfight with other guards, one robber was hit in the jaw with a shotgun blast, but the thieves escaped with the money anyway.

Police launched the biggest manhunt in Denver history. Shopkeepers closed up rather than accept stolen money. Bootleggers were shut down on the highways, and the price of booze skyrocketed. One psychic even predicted a robber would confess his crime in church.

A month later, the frozen body of the wounded robber—career criminal Nick "Chainsaw Jimmie" Trainor—was found in the getaway car, which had been dumped in the garage of a house at 1631 Gilpin St. (now a vacant lot at GPS 39.74239, -104.96732). Photos of Trainor's corpse were published in local papers, but he was only identified after his fingertips were stripped off and stretched to make prints. Great crowds of spectators gathered for his funeral at Riverside Cemetery (5201 Brighton Blvd.), and dozens volunteered as pallbearers for the celebrity crook. Trainor's unmarked grave is two graves west of a marker for Charles Kelly, in Section 4, Lot 7, Block 14, or GPS 39.79578, -104.96169.

Within weeks, police raided a Minnesota hideout and found $80,000 of the Mint's stolen $200,000—the only money ever recovered from the heist.

Twelve years later, Denver police claimed they had identified five men and two women who'd had roles in the robbery, all of

*One guard and one robber were killed in a
daring $200,000 robbery of the Denver Mint
in 1922.*

whom were either dead or in far-flung prisons on other charges.
Nobody was ever charged in the raid, and the Denver Police Department officially closed the case in 1934.

The 1922 robbery wasn't the Denver Mint's first. In 1920, a disgruntled Mint worker named Orville Harrington stole $100,000 worth of gold ingots—reportedly in his hollow wooden leg. He buried them in an orchard and in the cellar of his Denver house, but before he could melt them down, he was caught. Harrington was convicted and sentenced to ten years in prison, but he was paroled after only three and a half years.

JUSTICE BYRON "WHIZZER" WHITE'S GRAVE
Denver

St. John's Episcopal Cathedral is at 1350 Washington St. Justice White's ashes are entombed on the west side of All Soul's Walk, which is on the eastern side of the church, at GPS 39.73818, -104.97800.

Colorado native Byron Raymond White (1917–2002) led a storied life. An All-America halfback who graduated first in his high school, college, and law school classes. A Rhodes Scholar. A professional football player. A World War II hero. And a U.S. Supreme Court justice.

As a justice, White's voice loomed large in two of the most significant crime-and-punishment issues to come before the highest court in the past century: the Miranda rule and the constitutionality of the American death penalty.

Although appointed by President John F. Kennedy, a Democrat, White believed tougher law enforcement tactics made America safer. He dissented in the landmark 1966 *Miranda v. Arizona* case that established an arrested criminal's rights to remain silent, have a lawyer, etc. And when the constitutionality of capital punishment came under fire in *Furman v. Georgia,* White voted with the majority to strike down the death penalty in 1972 until new laws could be written to satisfy the Supreme Court's desire for less arbitrary death laws. Capital punishment, which had been suspended by states in a voluntary moratorium in 1965, resumed in 1977.

White retired in 1993 after thirty-one years on the Supreme Court, the fourth longest tenure in the twentieth century. The federal courthouse in Denver is named for White, who died April 15, 2002, at age eighty-four.

BOMBING OF UNITED 629
Denver

Always the dutiful son, **Jack Graham** lugged his mother's heavy luggage to Denver Stapleton International Airport so she could catch United 629 to Portland on November 1, 1955. But when a clerk told her that her bags were thirty-seven pounds too heavy and she'd have to pay an extra fee, Daisie King asked Jack if she should unpack some of her stuff.

"Mother, I'm sure you will need it," he insisted. Daisie paid the fee, kissed her son good-bye, and boarded the plane.

Eleven minutes after takeoff, United 629 crashed about thirty-two miles north of Denver, near Longmont, Colorado. All thirty-nine passengers and five crew members were killed.

Witnesses told federal investigators the plane seemed to explode in midair. So investigators gathered as many pieces of the shattered DC-6 wreckage as they could and reassembled it in a Denver warehouse, but no single piece was larger than an automobile. Evidence suggested a time bomb had exploded in the rear cargo bay—only the second known case of sabotage in American commercial aviation history.

Who would blow up a plane full of innocent people? FBI agents combed passenger lists, especially those who'd bought insurance. When they found **Daisie King**'s purse in the wreckage, it contained articles about her son Jack, a convicted forger and troublemaker. They discovered Jack had also collected insurance money after a mysterious explosion at his mother's East Denver hamburger stand less than a year before.

At Jack's house (2650 West Mississippi Ave. in Denver, or GPS 39.696611, -105.019963), FBI agents found bomb-making parts that matched debris at the crash, as well as six insurance policies on his mother that he'd bought at the airport on the day of the crash—all naming him as the beneficiary.

Jack had long held grudges against his mother. After his father died, he spent time in an orphanage until his mother remarried. He

Bomber Jack Graham

grew up a strange child who couldn't stay out of trouble but often dodged any serious punishment.

Before the crash, he told his wife he had a "little surprise" for his mother, and he was putting it in her luggage. In fact, it was twenty-five sticks of dynamite on a timer. He had hoped to collect tens of thousands of dollars on his mother's travel insurance and more than $100,000 from her estate—as well as evening the score on his old animosities against his mom.

He planned to detonate the plane over the rugged Rockies, but an unexpected delay in takeoff meant the plane blew up at eleven thousand feet just forty miles north of Denver.

He confessed the bombing to investigators. Although he later recanted, Jack Graham (1932–1957) was convicted in 1956 and sentenced to die. Before he was executed in the Colorado State Prison's gas chamber, he told a reporter, "As far as feeling any remorse for these people, I don't. I can't help it. Everybody pays their way and takes their chances. That's just the way it goes."

Daisie King (1902–1955) was buried at Denver's Fairmount Cemetery, 430 South Quebec St.; her grave is in Lot 135, Block 239, at GPS 39.70795, -104.89627. After her son's execution, his ashes were scattered around her grave.

The wreckage and bodies of United 629 were strewn for a mile across two family farms, six miles east of Longmont. A young priest with a flashlight walked among the scattered burning wreckage into the night, administering last rites to the mangled corpses. Most of the crash debris was along CO 66, about a mile east of modern-day I-25. The plane's tail section was found at about GPS 40.188016, -104.946556, near the southwest corner of CR 28 and Colorado Boulevard/CR 13. The debris field then stretched more than a mile northwest, with the engines landing at about GPS 40.196437, -104.956384, just northeast of the former Hopp farm on CR 11. This is all private property.

For many years, farmers in the area found silverware, eyeglasses and other grim reminders of the tragedy in the dirt.

The bombing of United 629—only the second proven case of an airline bombing over the U.S. mainland—remains the fifth deadliest mass murder in American history.

SKINHEADS' BUS STOP MURDER
Denver

This Denver Regional Transportation District (RTD) bus stop is at the eastern corner of 17th Street and Welton Avenue, or GPS 39.745509, -104.989895.

On the night of November 18, 1997, Senegalese immigrant **Oumar Dia** (1959–1997) was waiting for a bus home from his job as a downtown hotel bellhop when two neo-Nazi skinheads walked past. One of them, Nathan Thill, slapped Dia's hat from his head, called him a "nigger," and asked him if he was ready to die. Then he shot Dia four times while his companion watched. The thirty-eight-year-old husband and father of three died almost instantly.

A bystander, thirty-seven-year-old single mother and nurse's aide **Jeannie VanVelkinburgh,** tried to intervene, but she was shot in the spine, paralyzing her from the waist down.

Thill and his buddy were arrested later that night after Thill pulled the gun on another black man several blocks away.

Thill was convicted of murder and sentenced to life in prison without parole. His companion received a lighter sentence and was paroled in 2003.

Dia's body was sent home to his village in Senegal to be buried. VanVelkinburgh, who never worked again, had no insurance, so generous Denverites took up collections to pay her medical bills. Once hailed as a hero, she faded from the limelight, grew depressed, and seldom ventured out. Five years after the Dia shooting, VanVelkinburgh (1959–2002) committed suicide in her home.

Colorado Gov. Bill Owens attended VanVelkinburgh's funeral at Crown Hill Cemetery, 7777 West 29th Ave. in Wheat Ridge. Her grave is at GPS 39.76175, -105.08342.

"She's in a better place now," her brother said at her funeral. "Now, she's walking again."

MURDER AT THE BROWN PALACE
Denver
The hotel is at 321 17th St., or GPS 39.744102, -104.987787.

If she had lived in the celebrity-obsessed age of tabloid TV, **Isabel Springer** (1880–1917) might have been Lindsay Lohan, Paris Hilton, and Anna Nicole Smith all wrapped up in one sassy package.

In 1907, when beautiful divorcée Isabel married Denver millionaire **John W. Springer** (1859–1945)—twenty years older than Isabel—she moved into her husband's mansion at 930 Washington St. (now an apartment building at GPS 39.73106, -104.978523) and their apartment suite in the downtown Brown Palace hotel (Rooms 600 and 602). She quickly seduced the society pages of the local press, but that wasn't the least of her seductions. The manipulative Isabel kept up a romantic affair with an exciting beau—professional balloon-racer and bon vivant **Tony von Phul** (1878–1911) of St. Louis. Even after Isabel's marriage to another man, the reckless adventurer von Phul was often seen with her.

Enter **Frank Henwood** (1877–1929). Although he was a friend and business partner of her husband, the beguiling Isabel had soon cast her spell over Henwood too. The four-way tryst finally came to a head when Isabel summoned von Phul to Denver—and sent Henwood to retrieve some embarrassing letters she'd written to her amorous aeronaut.

On May 24, 1911, the two men met in the Marble Bar of the Brown Palace. Words were exchanged. Von Phul knocked Henwood to the floor. Henwood drew a pistol and fired six shots, mortally wounding an innocent bystander and von Phul, who died the next day.

Back in Missouri, von Phul was eulogized as a daring sportsman and buried with great pomp at Calvary Cemetery in St. Louis.

Henwood was convicted of murder and condemned to hang, but the Colorado governor commuted his sentence to life in prison, where he died in 1929 at age fifty-two. He was buried in a family plot in Jersey City, New Jersey.

John Springer divorced Isabel five weeks after the murder, even before her graphic letters were revealed at Henwood's trial. The alcoholic and cocaine-addicted Isabel died in 1917 in a Chicago charity ward and was buried in Fair View Cemetery in Fairview, New Jersey. She was only thirty-seven.

John Springer outlived them all, dying at age eighty-five in Littleton, Colorado, where he had established a ranch that would become one of Denver's most popular suburban neighborhoods, Highlands Ranch. He is buried with his last wife, Janette, under a blue spruce in the Littleton Cemetery, 6155 South Prince St. in Littleton. His grave is in Block 7, Lot 56, at GPS 39.60475, -105.01774.

Springer's Highlands Ranch Mansion—once called "Castle Isabel" after his young wife—still exists. The fourteen-bedroom, 22,000-square-foot estate is at the heart of modern-day Highlands Ranch at GPS 39.536316, -104.971265. It is being renovated to host community events in the future.

The Brown Palace's Marble Bar is still a bar inside the hotel; now it's known as Churchill's.

The case was explored in Dick Kreck's 2003 book *Murder at the Brown Palace.*

A high-society love quadrangle turned deadly at the elegant Brown Palace in 1911.

Isabel Springer

SERIAL KILLER'S BACKYARD CEMETERY
Denver

Richard Paul White's former home is at 2885 Albion St., or GPS 39.758011, -104.939569. This is private property.

In 2003, thirty-year-old former printer Richard Paul White had become a menace. He was planning a mass murder at his old workplace, but then he shot and killed a friend in a drunken rage. He fled into the Rockies armed only with a .40-caliber Glock pistol.

When a Denver SWAT team finally captured him at a remote camp, he admitted killing his friend—then shocked investigators by confessing to the rapes and murders of five other people, mostly Denver prostitutes. The corpses of two women—Victoria Lyn Turpin, thirty-two, and Annaletia Maria Gonzales, twenty-seven—were found buried in White's backyard at 2885 Albion St.

To avoid the death penalty, White later led investigators to two other buried bodies in southern Colorado. He is now serving several life sentences without the possibility of parole at the state prison in Cañon City.

White was eager to portray himself as a caring human when he told investigators he cried with his victims before he killed them. "I'm not a remorseless jerk. I'm kind of unique in that respect."

MURDER OF NFL'S DARRENT WILLIAMS
Denver

Williams's limo was sprayed by bullets while he was driving on Speer Boulevard near West 11th Ave., in the vicinity of GPS 39.732892, -104.992776.

At twenty-four, Denver Broncos cornerback Darrent Williams (1982–2007) was living his dream life. He had just finished his second season in the National Football League and was likely to be a starter in the coming season.

He and several teammates celebrated New Year's Eve at a now-defunct Denver club known as The Shelter (1037 N. Broadway, or GPS 39.73287, -104.98752). Some of Williams' entourage sprayed champagne that doused a few gangbangers in the crowd. A confrontation erupted and Williams tried unsuccessfully to intervene, so he and several friends then left in his Hummer limousine.

Less than a mile from the club, a passing SUV riddled the limo with bullets, hitting Williams in the neck and killing him. Police later found the SUV but couldn't pin a murder charge on anyone until almost two years later, when a Crips gang member named Willie Clark confessed. In 2010, gangbanger Clark was convicted of Williams's murder and sentenced to life in prison plus 1,152 years.

Darrent Williams was buried at in his hometown of Fort Worth, Texas. His grave is at Laurel Land-Fort Worth Cemetery, 7100 Crowley Rd., or GPS 32.64240, -97.34941.

In 2008, the Darrent Williams Memorial Teen Center was opened in Montbello by the Boys & Girls Clubs of Metro Denver at 4397 Crown Blvd., or GPS 39.779815, -104.839702. A heroic statue of Williams stands outside.

HAUNTED CHEESMAN PARK
Denver
Cheesman Park is at Franklin and 8th Streets and is open to the public from dawn to 11 p.m. GPS: 39.732793, -104.966555.

In the 1890s, imaginations across America were captured by the City Beautiful Movement, an urban beautification campaign that suggested the path to a lovely citizenry was lovely cities. Denver's city fathers, eager to transform their gritty Western cowtown into a great "white city," decided to start with the city's decrepit, 160-acre Mount Prospect Cemetery. The weedy, decaying

Mount Prospect had become an eyesore, and developers envisioned a grand space akin to Manhattan's Central Park. But to create "breathing spaces" for the living, they had to first remove the dead.

Mount Prospect had its own peculiar history. Its first two burials were said to be a local gambler and the man who murdered him in 1860. It was also the final resting place for most of the rugged city's marginal characters, such as hookers, scoundrels, and vagabonds.

In 1893, the city hired local undertaker **Edward P. McGovern** to remove thousands of unclaimed corpses from the graveyard, paying him $1.90 per body. McGovern made his macabre task even more macabre and profitable by ordering small, child-sized caskets and hacking cadavers into many pieces and placing them in several caskets—tripling or quadrupling his fee—or by simply filling coffins with dirt and rocks. Some say McGovern and his men also stole valuables from the buried bodies.

Ah, but the exhumation of old corpses was a form of public entertainment in the 19th century, so curious locals would gather to watch the morbid work. They soon reported McGovern's trickery to authorities, who immediately shut down the exhumation project and proclaimed that any loved ones who still remained in the cemetery after ninety days would rest forever in unmarked graves beneath the new park.

McGovern's chicanery drained the city's coffers, so work stopped for many years, leaving half-dug graves and tumbled headstones in a dangerous jumble. Fences were built around it to keep people from falling into the open graves, but children still found it to be a fascinating playground.

Among the "white city" movement's believers was **Robert Speer** (1855–1918), who became Denver's mayor in 1904 and immediately focused on the transformation of the wrecked Mount Prospect Cemetery. By 1910, it was a fresh, verdant urban park with public gardens, woodlands, ponds, paths, and neoclassical monuments—all in the city center. Nobody knows exactly how many people are still buried under Cheesman's tranquil lawns, but as recently as 2008, workers building a parking garage at the Denver Botanic Garden unearthed another unmarked grave—among hundreds still known to exist.

Today, Cheesman Park is considered by paranormal researchers to be among the world's greatest ghost-hunting sites.

Speer, a city-planning visionary for whom one of Denver's grandest boulevards was named, was buried in the prestigious Fairmount Cemetery, 430 South Quebec St. His grave is in Block 24, Lot 76, or GPS 39.70565, -104.89632.

The park was eventually named for **Walter S. Cheesman** (1838–1907), a successful (if slightly shady) entrepreneur whose postmortem reputation was improved when his widow donated $100,000 to the city for an elegant parthenon at the park. He is also buried at Fairmount Cemetery, and his grave is in Lot 16, Block A, at GPS 39.70702, -104.89999.

McGovern was never prosecuted, but he was forever tainted by the scandal. He died in 1925 and was buried—with all the proper rites—at Mount Olivet Cemetery, 12801 West 44th Ave. in Wheat Ridge. McGovern's grave is in Section 9, Block 9, Lot 8 (or GPS 39.78437, -105.14480).

Also see Pinkerton Legend James McParland's Grave (Wheat Ridge), Fairmount Cemetery (Denver).

MURDER AT RICHTHOFEN CASTLE
Denver

The historic mansion is at 7020 East 12th Ave. The shooting happened on the sidewalk in front of the easternmost front gate into the estate, at GPS 39.735567, -104.906285.

The 1911 murder trial of Gertrude Gibson Patterson was so lurid and salacious that a Denver women's club demanded local newspapers stop covering it—which they didn't, of course. It came just months after seductive socialite Isabel Springer was embroiled

Gertrude Patterson shot her husband to death just outside this gate to the once-posh mansion owned by relatives of the Red Baron.

in a murderous tryst that killed two men, and Patterson's case was touted as the "trial of the century" in Colorado.

Gertrude (b. 1881) was a small-town Illinois girl who went to the big city of Chicago when she turned eighteen. There she worked as a seamstress until she became the mistress of Emil W. Strouss, a Chicago millionaire "sugar daddy" who took her to Paris and sometimes called her "Mrs. Strouss." Strouss wanted to marry the pretty, young Gertrude and to pay for her education—but in the end, Gertrude decided instead to marry a dashing former football player named Charles Patterson.

Gertrude claimed Strouss gave Charles $1,500 to overlook her ongoing affair with Strouss, which he did. Suffering with tuberculosis, Charles was stung by his wife's infidelity, but he also enjoyed the money it was bringing him—even if he increasingly saw himself as a "pimp."

That's when the beatings began. Gertrude began to fear her husband's rages. They separated, and Charles moved into a tuberculosis sanatorium across the street from Denver's Richthofen Castle, a twenty-one-room mansion built by relatives of the German World War I flier who'd soon come to be known as the Red Baron, Manfred von Richthofen.

On the morning of September 27, 1911, Charles and Gertrude were walking briskly down 12th Avenue, arguing over money. Eyewitnesses saw Charles slug Gertrude. She pulled a pistol from her purse and fired four shots at Charles in front of the Richthofen Castle's front gate, then ran across the expansive lawn into the estate. Two bullets hit him in the back, and he died. He was buried in Chicago.

Gertrude faced murder charges in one of the most sensational trials in Denver history. While the prosecutor called her a "vile vampire" who manipulated and enslaved men, her defenders were blaming her wife-beating pimp of a husband for his demise. The modern-day battered-woman defense was getting a test run in 1911. Through it all, the beautiful, charming Gertrude openly flirted with jurors.

She was acquitted. After the trial, at least four of the male jurors visited her in her hotel, bearing gifts and flowers, but Gertrude soon disappeared. The next year, 1912, newspapers reported that she had died under an assumed name aboard the RMS *Titanic* when it sank, but enterprising reporters later said they found her living in luxury in Chicago, perhaps still with the blessing of the elderly Emil Strouss.

The case is examined in Robert Hardaway's 2003 book *Alienation of Affection.*

See also Murder at the Brown Palace (Denver).

BOETTCHER KIDNAPPING
Denver
The millionaire's mansion was at 777 Washington St., now an apartment building on the southwest corner of 8th and Washington Streets, at GPS 39.728742, -104.978914

The Boettcher family was instrumental in Denver's formative years, profiting enormously from lucrative real estate and business holdings. But over the years, the family's wealth has occasionally been a curse.

A little before midnight on February 12, 1933, Charles Boettcher II—grandson of the family's patriarch, Charles—was kidnapped in the mansion's garage. The kidnappers handed his wife a ransom note for $60,000 and fled.

The Boettchers agreed to pay the ransom, even as the fledgling FBI tried desperately to solve the case.

The kidnappers were a couple of pioneering outlaws, Verne Sankey and Gordon Alcorn, who had given up robbing banks to try kidnapping-for-profit. They got so good at it that other outlaws copied them—most notably George "Machine Gun" Kelly with his abduction of Oklahoma millionaire Charles Urschel.

Just before the ransom was paid, Sankey and Alcorn released Charles Boettcher II from the South Dakota farmhouse where they'd kept him for seventeen days. Two minor cohorts were busted when they picked up the ransom; Sankey and Alcorn became two of America's most wanted fugitives until they were captured several months later. Some $9,000 of the ransom money was found buried in coffee cans around the farmhouse.

Before trial, Sankey hanged himself with a necktie in his South Dakota jail cell; Alcorn and his accomplices went to federal prison for life.

Charles Boettcher II died of a heart attack in San Francisco in 1963, the same year the mansion was leveled to build a high-rise apartment building. He was sixty-one and is buried in the family's crypt in Fairmount Cemetery, 430 South Quebec St., in the Mausoleum's Chapel Floor, at GPS 39.70518, -104.89397.

See also Adolph Coors III Kidnapping and Murder (Morrison); Riverside Cemetery (Denver); Millionaire's Hit-and-Run Victim (Golden).

"DOG THE BOUNTY HUNTER" CHILDHOOD HOME
Denver
The house is at 75 South Vrain, or GPS 39.715385, -105.0459.

The world's most famous bounty hunter, **Duane "Dog" Chapman** (b. 1953), was born in Denver and grew up in his parents Wesley and Barbara's modest suburban house on the city's west side. As a teenager in the 1960s, Duane started getting in neighborhood trouble that led ultimately to a 1976 Texas murder charge and prison time. After finding Jesus in prison, Chapman emerged to eventually become a bounty hunter and reality-TV star. Whether he's born-again or just TV make-believe, it's been more than thirty years since Chapman's last felony arrest—tempests over possibly illegal Mexican forays and angry racial slurs notwithstanding.

See also Bobby Brown Bail Bonds (Colorado Springs).

UNITED BANK ROBBERY AND MURDERS
Denver
The fifty-story downtown bank building, now known as the Wells Fargo Center, is on the northeast corner of Lincoln Street and East 17th Ave., or GPS 39.743464, -104.985893.

Father's Day 1991 was a quiet Sunday, not a big day for either banking or bank robbers. But that morning, while six bank workers were in the cash-counting room deep inside the towering United Bank of Denver, a robber killed four unarmed guards with eighteen shots from a .38-caliber handgun and over the next twenty minutes stole $200,000 in small bills—leaving more than $2 million behind.

Two weeks later, police arrested James W. King, a retired Denver police sergeant and married father of three children who had also worked as a part-time security guard at United Bank.

A lone robber killed four guards and escaped with $200,000 in a 1991 robbery at the towering United Bank in downtown Denver. The money has never been recovered and the robber never caught.

The FBI built an impressive case against King, amassing six hundred pages of evidence, including a book he was writing about bank security flaws. Plus, the killer had slipped through a labyrinth of security obstacles and retrieved several surveillance videos, suggesting he was familiar with the bank's system.

But a jury couldn't connect all the dots. King was acquitted in 1992.

The murder weapon and the money have never been recovered.

One of the slain guards, Phillip Mankoff (1949–1991), was buried at Congregation Emanuel Cemetery (inside Fairmount Cemetery) at 430 South Quebec St. The grave is in Section 37, Row 142, Grave 2, or GPS 39.70497, -104.90150.

INSIDER TRADING SCANDAL
Denver
Qwest Communications International's headquarters is at 1801 California St., or GPS 39.747443, -104.989804

By August 2002, telecom giant Qwest's stock had tanked. In only three months, it plunged from $38 a share to $2. So amid rumors of a massive $3 billion insider-trading scam, Qwest CEO Joe Nacchio quit.

In 2005, Nacchio was indicted on forty-two counts of insider trading stemming from his sale of $39 million worth of stock just before the price plunged. In 2007, he was convicted on nineteen counts and ordered to pay $71 million in fines and forfeited profits. In 2009, after a series of appeals and legal maneuvers, he reported to a Pennsylvania federal prison to serve six years for his crimes, which were among a spate of mega-dollar white-collar scandals at other companies like Enron and Global Crossing.

BURGLARS WITH BADGES
Denver

On patrol one night in April 1960, Denver Police Officer John D. Bates saw a curious thing: A safe fell out of two fleeing burglars' car. So he waited to see who'd pick it up. Surprisingly, the man who showed up was a fellow cop.

Bates had already heard the rumors that at least a dozen cops were involved in Denver burglaries, often while they were on duty. When he told his chief, he was ordered to get psychiatric counseling.

But when suspended Denver Police Department Patrolman Arthur Winstanley was busted on Christmas night 1960—his second burglary arrest in six months—the whole story spilled out. Denver's widespread police burglary ring became international news.

For months, several rings of DPD officers had been breaking into local businesses and scoring big, including a $40,000 burglary at a local Safeway in which the burglars had used milk from the cooler to cool their safe-cracking saw.

Cops in cruisers usually cased their targets while other cops stood watch. When the break-ins began, the lookouts monitored police radios for alarm calls. The next day, the same cops usually returned to investigate, often destroying leftover evidence. (In one case, the shopkeeper found a pair of police trousers at the scene. The pants were taken as evidence ... and vanished.)

By the end of 1961, forty-seven Denver-area policemen had been arrested, and a sheriff, two deputies, two private detectives, and a civilian were implicated in the burglary ring. Denver's police chief was forced to resign in disgrace.

Officer Bates, fifty-two, who had tried unsuccessfully to report the crimes to bosses who didn't believe him (or were covering up), was briefly accused by an angry fellow cop but cleared of any involvement. He retired from the force and died in 1981. He is buried at Mount Olivet Cemetery, 12801 West 44th Ave. in Wheat Ridge. His unmarked grave is in Section 27, Block 11, or GPS 39.78042, -105.14982.

The highest-ranking officer charged, Sergeant Hobert W. Lamont, forty-seven, pleaded guilty and did prison time. He died in 1987 and is buried at Fairview Cemetery on Cemetery Road, a quarter mile east of Basalt, Colorado. His grave is at GPS 39.36458, -107.02119.

Dishonored cop Arthur Winstanley self-published a 2009 book about the scandal, *Burglars in Blue.*

FAIRMOUNT CEMETERY
Denver

Fairmount Cemetery is at 430 South Quebec St., or GPS 39.708536, -104.903276.

Since 1890, the 280-acre Fairmount Cemetery has become the final resting place for many of Denver's most notable citizens. Governors, senators, industrialists, philanthropists, and brilliant academics are buried here—and so are a wide variety of criminals, victims, lawmen, and other people whose lives were defined by crime and scandal. Among them:

- Con man **Lou Blonger** (1849–1924), the politically connected kingpin of widespread bunco rackets in Colorado. Operating out of his Elite saloon at 1628 Stout St. (no longer existent) with his brother, Sam, Lou was the king of Denver's blossoming underworld, with gaming houses, saloons, and plenty of important people in his pocket. In 1892, the Blongers bought the Forest Queen Mine above Cripple Creek (GPS 38.746667, -105.140833), whose riches they shared with several influential "partners." Their unmolested decades of crime ended when a young district attorney, **Philip Van Cise** (1884–1969)—who'd refused the Blongers' "help" in the election—bypassed the usual legal channels and arrested the Blongers. Lou was convicted and sent to prison, where he died on April 20, 1924. His grave is in Lot 26, Block 63, at GPS 39.70897, -104.90104.

  Van Cise is buried at Fort Logan National Cemetery, 4400 West Kenyon; his grave is in Section R-1633, or at GPS 39.64738, -105.05248. Today's Denver County Jail bears his name.

- **Dr. J. G. Locke** (1871–1935), Grand Wizard of the Ku Klux Klan in Denver in the 1920s who organized boycotts of Jewish stores. His crypt is in Lot 22, Block 63, at GPS 39.70941, -104.90102.

- Madam **Mattie Silks** (1846–1929), Denver's most famous brothel-keeper, who reportedly was never a prostitute herself. Her House of Mirrors, 1942 Market St. (GPS 39.75327,

Madam Mattie Silks's bordello at 2009 Market Street is a historic Denver landmark today.

-104.99414), was deemed the most elegant of Colorado's bordellos and was restored in 1998 as a restaurant with an upstairs bar and museum. Her sporting house at 2009 Market St. (GPS 39.7539, -104.993314), now a lawyer's office, is also preserved as a Denver historic landmark. She is buried under the name Martha Ready in Lot 131, Block 12, at GPS 39.70846, -104.89719.

- Reporter **Polly Pry** (1857–1938) was a groundbreaking investigative reporter at the *Denver Post* at a time when newspapering wasn't considered a woman's work. The target of one bombing and a shooting, she vehemently opposed union leader Mother Jones and worked as a war correspondent during Pancho Villa's rebellion and World War I. Her interviews with cannibal Alfred "Alferd" Packer led to his early release. She is buried under her real name, Leonel Ross Anthony O'Bryan, in Block 23, Lot 179, at GPS 39.70579, -104.89739.

- Mayor **Wolfe Londoner** (1842–1912) was the first and only Denver mayor forced to resign because of election fraud— reportedly for stuffing ballot boxes with the help of bunco man Lou Blonger, lawman Bat Masterson, and crime boss Soapy Smith. He is buried in Lot 71, Block 24, at GPS 39.70572, -104.89646.

- Columbine victim **Isaiah Shoels** (1980–1999) is in Lot 54, Block 68, at GPS 39.70541, -104.89217.

- Airplane bomber **Jack Graham** and his victim mother **Daisie King** are buried here in Lot 135, Block 39, at GPS 39.70795, -104.89627.

- Millionaire kidnapping victim **Charles Boettcher II** (1902–1963) is in the family mausoleum at GPS 39.70518, -104.89397.

- Pioneering educator **Emily Griffith** (1868–1947) and sister **Florence** (1881–1947), who were both murdered, are buried in Block 61, Lot 27, or GPS 39.71014, -104.90068.

- **Arthur L. Collins** (1868–1902), well known as a strict mine manager, was shot to death in his home on the Smuggler-Union Mine property near Telluride by unknown assailants in the aftermath of a violent union strike. His grave is in Lot 112, Block 2, at GPS 39.70850, -104.89931.

- **Silas Soule** and Colorado **Gov. John Evans**—key figures in the 1864 Sand Creek Massacre—are buried here. See their listings under that crime in Colorado's Front Range chapter.

See also Sand Creek Massacre of 1864 (Sand Creek); Cannibal Camp (Lake City); Bombing of United 629 (Denver); Emily Griffith Murder (Pinecliffe); Boettcher Kidnapping (Denver); Mass Murder at Columbine (Littleton).

HISTORY COLORADO CENTER
Denver
In 2012, the new museum will open at 1200 Broadway, or GPS 39.735396, -104.987192. Check www.coloradohistory.org for hours, research rules, and admission fees.

The Colorado Historical Society operates one of the Rockies' most fascinating museums and libraries. Among the items available for researchers to examine are:

- Material related to the court-martial of Pfc. Dale Maple, an American guard at a Colorado POW camp who helped two Nazi prisoners escape. Maple was the first WWII American soldier to be convicted of treason. His death sentence was later commuted to life in prison at Fort Leavenworth.

- A gun related to Alfred Packer's cannibalism scandal.

- Materials related to the 1933 Charles Boettcher II kidnapping.

- Crime scrapbooks of early Denver lawman Sam Howe.

RIVERSIDE CEMETERY
Denver

Riverside Cemetery is at 5201 Brighton Blvd., or GPS 39.789391, -104.963078.

Opened in 1876, Riverside Cemetery is Denver's oldest grave-yard and comprises more than sixty-seven thousand graves. Like its sister cemetery, Fairmount, Riverside contains many notables, including crime-related figures. Among them:

- Flamboyant lawyer **Ben Laska** (d. 1948), who unsuccess-fully defended "Machine Gun" Kelly's cohort Albert Bates in their 1935 Charles Urschel kidnapping case. Laska—who sometimes used magic tricks in court—was later con-victed of accepting ransom money for his services and sent to Fort Leavenworth prison for six years. He was pardoned by President Harry Truman in 1947 shortly before he com-mitted suicide with sleeping pills while seeking reinstate-ment to the Colorado bar. His ashes are presumed to have been buried among the cemetery's cremains behind the main office at GPS 39.790193, -104.96207.

- **Wilson E. Sisty** (d. 1889), who became Denver's first official marshal in 1859—shortly after the city's first murder. His grave is in Lot 16, Block 5, at GPS 39.79235, -104.96211.

- Lawman **David J. Cook** (1840–1907) was a former Union spy who founded the Rocky Mountain Detective Association, the first formal network of cops west of the Mississippi. He arrested (or killed) more than three thousand criminals, including members of the notorious Musgrove-Franklin Gang. In 1882, Cook published a memoir he called *Hands Up! or Twenty Years of Detective Work in the Mountains and on the Plains.* His grave is in Lot 70, Block 15, at GPS 39.79253, -104.96306.

- Robber **Nick Trainor,** killed in the 1922 Denver Mint Robbery. Trainor's funeral was a widely attended affair, and many bystanders volunteered to act as pallbearers. His unmarked grave is in Section 4, Lot 7, Block 14, or GPS 39.79578, -104.96169.

- Immigrant and Korean freedom fighter **Park Hee Byung** (1871–1907) was assassinated and buried in an unmarked grave here. But in 2003, South Korean scholars located the grave and erected a $3,000 monument to Park's accomplishments. His grave is GPS 39.79644, -104.96049.

- Several key figures in the 1864 Sand Creek Massacre are buried here.

See also Denver Mint Robbery (Denver); Sand Creek Massacre (Sand Creek).

MASS MURDER AT COLUMBINE
Littleton
The school is at 6201 South Pierce St., or GPS 39.604452, -105.07341.

Columbine wasn't the first school shooting in American history, nor even the deadliest. But it has clung to the American consciousness as one of the most symbolic mass murders of our time and certainly one of Colorado's worst tragedies.

On April 20, 1999, two senior boys—Dylan Klebold and Eric Harris—mounted a school attack that began as a terror bombing but quickly devolved into a forty-nine-minute shooting spree when the bombs failed. They literally planned to kill thousands to avenge myriad snubs that were both real and imagined.

The deeply disturbed pair plotted their attack for more than a year. They built more than one hundred bombs and cajoled friends into buying them guns. If all went according to plan, huge propane bombs would explode in the school cafeteria and kitchen, and the suicidal pair would shoot any survivors who ran outside. Other bombs were planted to kill first-responders.

Just after 11 a.m. on April 20, Harris and Klebold hauled their bombs into the school and waited outside for the Oklahoma City–style explosion. But it fizzled.

Armed with a pistol, a rifle, and two sawed-off shotguns, the two teens stormed the building, throwing pipe bombs and Molotov cocktails, and killing everyone they saw. The greatest slaughter was in the school library, where they played games of peekaboo with hiding students.

At 12:08, the two killers went to a corner of the library where they shot themselves, Harris in the mouth and Klebold in the head. Ironically, Harris was wearing a T-shirt that said *Natural Selection.*

When it was over, thirteen people were dead, twenty-four were wounded, and an entire nation suddenly feared its children could be killed in any classroom in any town.

The bloodshed at Littleton's Columbine High School in 1999 remains an open wound for the school, the city, and the nation.

Media reported that Harris and Klebold had been relentlessly bullied; were antisocial Goths who called themselves the Trenchcoat Mafia; were taking antidepressants; targeted jocks, blacks and Christians; and even asked one girl if she believed in God before shooting her. None of it was true, just part of the instant mythology that sprang up around the rampage. In fact, the pair had bragged in their own journals about harassing freshmen and "fags."

The attack changed school security and police tactics and provided an object lesson in leaping to judgment. It also proved to be sickly inspiration: Virginia Tech shooter Seung-Hui Cho praised "martyrs like Eric and Dylan" before he killed thirty-two people in 2007.

Harris and Klebold were cremated and their ashes given to their families.

Their victims were buried in various Denver-area cemeteries. **Kyle Velasquez** and **Steven Curnow,** who'd both planned to enlist after graduation, were buried at Fort Logan National Cemetery. They are buried side by side in Section V, Site 2237, or GPS 39.64639, -105.04561.

Isaiah Shoels, the only black victim, was buried at Denver's Fairmount Cemetery in Lot 54, Block 68, at GPS 39.70541, -104.89217.

Lauren Townsend and **Daniel Rohrbaugh** were buried not far apart in Littleton Cemetery. Townsend is at GPS 39.60298, -105.01775; Rohrbaugh is at GPS 39.60275, -105.01799.

Cassie Bernall is in the Golden Cemetery's City Section, just south of the intersection of Frontier and Pathfinder Paths, or GPS 39.73057, -105.19563.

Daniel Mauser, Kelly Fleming, and **Matthew Kechter** were buried in Mount Olivet Cemetery in Wheat Ridge. See their listings under that entry.

Corey dePooter, Rachel Scott, and teacher **Dave Sanders** are all in Chapel Hill Memorial Gardens in Centennial. DePooter and Scott are buried side by side in the Columbine Memorial section at GPS 39.60139, -104.94952. Sanders is buried in Section 394, or GPS 39.60094, -104.94704.

John Tomlin was buried in St. Peters Cemetery in Waterford, Wisconsin.

Memorials were erected in Robert Clement Park near the campus of Columbine High School at GPS 39.60529, -105.07873, and in Chapel Hill Memorial Gardens, 6601 South Colorado Blvd., in Centennial, at GPS 39.601389, -104.949444.

Several books cover the crime. Most recent is Dave Cullen's 2009 book *Columbine.*

PINKERTON LEGEND JAMES MCPARLAND'S GRAVE
Wheat Ridge

Mount Olivet Cemetery is at 12801 West 44th Ave. The grave is in Section 2, Block 1A, Lot O, Grave 3, or GPS 39.78369, -105.14489.

Irish-born **James McParland** (1843–1919) was running a liquor store in Chicago when he lost everything in the Great Chicago Fire of 1871. With no prospects and no money, he joined the Pinkerton Detective Agency—and over the next 50 years proved to be the most celebrated detective of his day.

His storied career began when he infiltrated the Molly Maguires, a secret militant gang of Irish coal miners plotting assassinations and violence against anti-union mine owners in 1870s Pennsylvania. Eventually, McParland gathered enough evidence to break up the organization; but also to prevent vengeful violence, ten Molly Maguires were hanged and several anti-union reprisals thwarted.

McParland's celebrity was bigger than reality. He was so famous that Sir Arthur Conan Doyle contrived a meeting between McParland and the fictional sleuth Sherlock Holmes in his 1915 novel *The Valley of Fear.*

After McParland was sent to Denver to manage all of Pinkerton's Western investigations, his career—and his reputation—grew. He cracked the case of the largest gold bullion theft in U.S. history and uncovered a plot to blow up a Kansas county's records vault to hide fraudulent mortgages. He also worked closely with famed cowboy detective Charlie Siringo.

In 1905, McParland investigated the bomb assassination of former Idaho Gov. Frank Steunenberg, a devoutly anti-union politician. The detective suspected high-ranking union officials of ordering the hit, but all were eventually acquitted—McParland's only real "failure."

McParland died May 18, 1919, in Denver's Mercy Hospital. Newspaper eulogies pointed out that the Great Detective (as he was known by Sherlock Holmes) had been the target of bombers, gunmen, arsonists, and a variety of other assassins, but persisted. "There's no romance in the life of a detective," McParland once said. "It's just work. Hard, hard work. That's all."

Also in Mount Olivet Cemetery:

- Graves for three victims of the 1999 Columbine shooting. **Daniel Mauser** is in Section 34, Block 5, or GPS 39.78037, -105.15240. **Kelly Fleming** is buried beneath a large white angel (surrounded by columbine flowers) in Section 34,

Block 4, or GPS 39.78028, -105.15218. **Matthew Kechter** is in Section 31, Block 7, or GPS 39.77955, -105.14763.

- **Joe Corbett** (1928–2009), who kidnapped and murdered brewery heir Adolph Coors III in 1960. His unmarked grave is beside a stone for "Kusner" in Section 28, Block 12, or GPS 39.78223, -105.14192.

- **Edward P. McGovern** (d. 1925), who scandalized Denver when he dug up the corpses under modern-day Cheesman Park. His grave is in Section 9, Block 9, Lot 8, or GPS 39.78437, -105.14480.

See also Haunted Cheesman Park (Denver); Adolph Coors III Kidnapping and Murder (Morrison); Mass Murder at Columbine (Littleton).

DENVER'S BROTHER HOODS
Wheat Ridge
Crown Hill Cemetery is at 7777 West 29th Ave.

Sometimes "family" is just a bunch of relatives … and sometimes it's something else.

In the 1920s, three Smaldone brothers—Eugene, aka "Checkers"; Clyde, aka "Flip Flop"; and Clarence, aka "Chauncey"—began their criminal careers as bootleggers. But the enterprising siblings soon caught the eyes of Colorado mobsters and rose through the ranks to the upper echelons of the Mile-High Mafia.

From Prohibition-era bootlegging to gangster-era violence to gambling rackets in the 1980s, the Smaldones are recognized as Colorado's First Family of organized crime. By 1930, the brothers had more than twenty-five arrests among them—and they were just getting started.

In 1933, when mobster Joseph Roma was shot fourteen times in a gangland execution, the Smaldones started their rise to power, taking over the "family" in the 1970s.

Gaetano's, a restaurant that advertises "Italian to die for," was the headquarters for Denver's mob underworld for decades.

Their base of operations was a family restaurant named Gaetano's at 3760 Tejon in Denver (GPS 39.769164, -105.011106), an Italian eatery with a bulletproof front door. Police believe the brothers stashed more than $200,000 in their basement office, from which they loaned $30,000 a day at 5 percent interest—a week. The restaurant (now owned by its employees) is still open.

Eugene (1911–1992) was the brains behind the gang. Suspected of playing a role in several killings, Eugene was never indicted for murder. He died at age eighty-one of a heart attack. He's buried in the Tower of Memories' Chapel Floor at GPS 39.758453, -105.092747.

Clyde (1906–1998) did plenty of prison time, including a stretch for an attempted bombing murder. In 1953, Clyde and Eugene were convicted of jury tampering after a gambling bust. In 1967, Clyde and others were busted for running a $100,000 a week bookmaking operation. Clyde died in a nursing home at age ninety-one. He was buried at Crown Hill's Garden Mausoleum Building 1 (Tier E) at GPS 39.76081, -105.08330.

Brother Clarence died in 2006 and was cremated.

The "family" history is explored in Dick Kreck's 2009 book *Smaldone: The Untold Story of an American Crime Family.*

Also in Crown Hill Cemetery: Mobsters **Sam Carlino** (1891–1931), **Pete Carlino** (1887–1931), and **Joseph Roma** (1895–1933), rivals who controlled two Colorado Mafia families.

The war started when the Pueblo-based Carlinos tried to muscle in on Roma's Denver turf. The strategy was fatal: Sam Carlino was shot to death in his home. A few months later, Pete Carlino, known as the "Al Capone of Colorado," was murdered in September 1931 and his bullet-riddled body stuffed under a bridge—until his killers moved it to be more easily discovered.

That left Roma—nicknamed "Little Caesar" because he was only five-foot-one—as the capo of Colorado crime. But on February 18, 1933, Roma was murdered gangland-style, too, although his killers were never identified.

Ironically, Roma and the Carlino brothers are all buried very close to each other on the first floor of Mount Olivet's Tower of Memories mausoleum at GPS 39.758436, -105.092576.

- **Kaysi Dawn McLeod** (1983–2003) is one of four known victims of serial killer Scott Lee Kimball, her mother's one-time boyfriend who has claimed he killed "dozens." In 2008, a hunter found McLeod's skull and other bones in a remote area of northwest Colorado. Her grave is in Block 16, Lot 21, or GPS 39.75937, -105.08565.

- Heroic bystander **Jeannie VanVelkinburgh** (1961–2002), who tried to stop the racist murder of a black man in downtown Denver, is buried in Block 13, Lot 186, or GPS 39.76175, -105.08342.

See also Skinheads' Bus Stop Murder (Denver).

Colorado Front Range

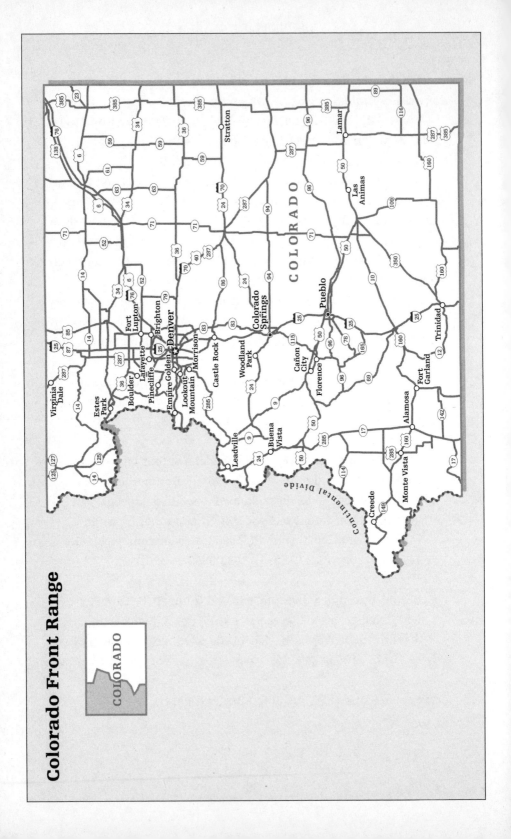

2

COLORADO FRONT RANGE

GANGSTER LLOYD BARKER'S GRAVE
Brighton

Elmwood Cemetery is at 14800 Old Brighton Rd. The unmarked grave is in Section 6, Block 40, or about GPS 39.96448, -104.83136.

Lloyd William "Red" Barker (1898–1949) was the second of four unsavory sons born to Arizona Barker—better known as gangster matriarch Ma Barker. FBI Director J. Edgar Hoover once called the Barkers "the toughest gang of hoodlums the FBI has ever been called upon to eliminate."

Busted for a 1921 mail truck robbery in Kansas, Lloyd served sixteen years at Leavenworth. While he was in prison, Ma Barker and her other criminal sons—Doc, Freddie, and Herman—all died violently. After being paroled, Lloyd enlisted as a cook at a POW camp during World War II and served honorably. After the war, Lloyd moved to the Denver suburb of Westminster, Colorado, and became manager of the Denargo Grill (which no longer exists at Broadway and 29th Street in Denver, or GPS 39.764591, -104.987197) in an attempt to go straight.

But after work on March 18, 1949, Lloyd was unlocking the back door of his little house at 3426 West 73rd Ave. in Westminster (GPS 39.829462, -105.031716) when his wife, Jean, shot him in the neck with a 20-gauge shotgun, killing him instantly. She was committed to an insane asylum.

The citizens of Westminster later embraced the memory of Lloyd Barker with a modest sidewalk plaque in the 3800 block of West 73rd Avenue at GPS 39.82913, -105.038783.

At his funeral, he was remembered as "the only one of Ma's boys who ever did an honest day's work." Buried in a grave that remains unmarked, Lloyd's exact final spot has been lost by the cemetery, but the likeliest spot is beside the grave of James and Cora Nelms.

See also Deputy Arthur Osborn's Grave (Pine Bluffs).

JONBENÉT RAMSEY MURDER
Boulder

The former Ramsey house is at 749 15th St. (originally 755), or GPS 40.00116, -105.27377.

Early on the morning after Christmas in 1996, a frantic Patsy Ramsey called 911 to report that JonBenét, her six-year-old daughter, was missing and a three-page ransom note demanding $118,000 had been found. Police rushed to the Ramsey home and began searching for JonBenét, who was found dead eight hours later in the basement by her father, John Ramsey. She had been severely beaten, bound, and strangled. Although she had not been raped, unidentified male DNA was later found in a blood sample on the little girl's panties.

And that's how one of the most controversial and confounding murder cases in American history began.

Suspicion immediately fell on the Ramsey family, including JonBenét's nine-year-old brother, Burke.

At first, police theorized Patsy had grievously hurt JonBenét in a fit of rage after she wet her bed on Christmas night and then killed her to cover it up. Then there were theories that father John had been having an incestuous relationship with his daughter, or Burke had accidentally killed her during rough play.

The mystery had elements of sex and wealth too. Reporters were fascinated by JonBenét's precocious participation in beauty pageants—and her mother's obsession with it. Millionaire John Ramsey had founded Access Graphics, a billion-dollar-a-year

The 1925 house where precocious JonBenét
Ramsey died in 1996 attracted so many
gawkers that its address was quietly
changed from 755 15th Street to 749.

computer distributor later bought by Lockheed, which kept him as
the CEO.

But police errors, political infighting, a nationwide media cir-
cus, and wild finger-pointing stymied the investigation. A grand jury
couldn't indict anyone, but the Ramseys remained under suspicion
for years, although they consistently argued JonBenét was killed by
an intruder. In 2008, new DNA tests cleared the entire Ramsey family of involvement.

In 2006, a former teacher and pedophile named John Mark Karr confessed to killing JonBenét, but investigators quickly proved he had nothing to do with her death. The prevailing theory today is that the killer was an intruder.

Patsy Ramsey, forty-nine, died of ovarian cancer in 2006 and is buried beside JonBenét in St. James Episcopal Cemetery in Marietta, Georgia.

The Ramseys' former Tudor-style home in a chic Boulder neighborhood has been bought and sold a few times since the murder, always at below-market prices because of the murder's stigma. The address was changed a few years after the killing, partly to confuse gawkers and partly to erase some of the shame.

In the meantime, the case remains unsolved.

JANE DOE HAS A NAME
Boulder

Columbia Cemetery is at 9th and Pleasant Streets. The grave is in Section B, Lot 15, or GPS 40.008991, -105.283568.

Sometimes a case isn't solved by cops but by civilians who can't let it go.

On April 8, 1954, some college kids found the body of a young woman beside Boulder Creek, eight miles west of town (GPS 40.00385, -105.40340). The battered body, partially eaten by animals, was so badly damaged her face was unidentifiable and her fingerprints were gone.

The coroner estimated she was seventeen to twenty years old, about five-foot-three and one hundred pounds. She had light brown hair and perfect teeth, but her eyes were gone. Her abdomen bore an appendectomy scar. She had been beaten then rolled over an embankment a week before she was found.

Sympathetic locals paid for a burial plot in the cemetery and a headstone that said only: JANE DOE, APRIL 1954, AGE ABOUT 20 YEARS.

Unidentified murder victim Jane Doe lay in this grave for more than fifty years before a local historian helped give her a real name.

More than forty years later, a local historian named Silvia Pettem got interested in Jane Doe's case. In 1996, she began labor-intensive research into other possible murder victims—and her likely killer.

After seeing a TV show in which an unidentified victim was exhumed, Pettem asked Boulder County cops to exhume Jane Doe. She started a nonprofit foundation to raise money for the research and enlisted several forensics experts to help.

In 2004—the murder's fiftieth anniversary—Jane Doe was exhumed and her DNA sampled. The investigation hit several dead ends over the next four years, including finding one of the most likely "victims" still alive in an Australian nursing home.

In 2008, an unexpected e-mail to Pettem's website yielded even more unexpected results. A woman wondered if Jane Doe might be her relative, who disappeared in 1954. DNA matched, and Jane Doe finally had a name: **Dorothy Gay Howard,** who had disappeared from her Phoenix, Arizona, home at age eighteen in March 1954.

Police credited Pettem's persistence with identifying Howard. A new marker was erected at her grave in May 2010, when Howard received a second funeral.

The killer has not been as assertively identified. He is believed to be Denver serial killer **Harvey Glatman,** who had attacked another woman in Boulder around the time of Howard's murder. He was living at the time with his mother in Denver's Capitol Hill district (1133 Kearney St., or GPS 39.73454, -104.91733), not far from Howard's aunt. Known as the Lonely Hearts Killer, Glatman (1927–1959) was executed at California's San Quentin Prison for three similar crimes. He is buried in the San Quentin Prison Cemetery.

Silvia Pettem described the case in her 2009 book *Someone's Daughter: In Search of Justice for Jane Doe.*

Also in Columbia Cemetery:

- Lawman and outlaw **Tom Horn** (1860–1903), one of the most legendary figures in Old West history, buried here by relatives after his hanging in Cheyenne, Wyoming. His grave is in Section C, Lot 74, or GPS 40.00751, -105.28355. See his entry under Outlaw/Lawman Tom Horn (Cheyenne).

DISC-SPORT PIONEER'S MURDER
Boulder

The former Bennigan's restaurant (now a different eatery) is at 2600 Canyon Blvd., near the entrance to The Village shopping center, at GPS 40.017216, -105.260321.

Henry Callahan (1957–1982) was a pioneer in the sport of Ultimate, a disc game that melds elements of soccer and football, played in forty-two countries. Callahan was a player who introduced the sport at the University of Oregon and cofounded the Ultimate team known as the Dark Star Alliance.

After visiting his brother in Boulder, the rootless Callahan decided to stay. He became headwaiter at the local Bennigan's restaurant and hoped to become a manager. But on June 23, 1982, a heroin addict and career criminal named Robert Wieghard walked into the restaurant and demanded money. Callahan gave him the cash, but for reasons unknown, Wieghard shot Callahan in the head anyway. Wieghard was convicted and is serving a life sentence, although he occasionally comes up for parole.

Half of Callahan's ashes traveled with his team to several tournaments for years after his death, and the urn was sometimes placed on the field in place of a live player. The team often scattered a small bit of his ashes on the fields where they played, and what wasn't scattered remains in the care of one of his former teammates in Eugene, Oregon.

COCKEYED LIZ'S GRAVE
Buena Vista

Mount Olivet Cemetery is a quarter mile southwest of Buena Vista on the Tin Cup lane. The grave is in Block A, Lot 12, or GPS 38.83663, -106.14635.

Elizabeth Spurgeon Enderlin (1857–1929) was one of Colorado's most colorful madams. Because of a childhood accident that damaged one of her eyes, she was known mostly by her nickname "Cockeyed Liz."

Lizzie became a prostitute at age thirteen. She came to Buena Vista in 1886 and opened her own whorehouse, the Palace Manor, at 428 East Main St. (GPS 38.84316, -106.12812). It still stands today, although it is a private home now.

In 1897, she married the town plumber, Alphonse "Foozy" Enderlin, and gave up the brothel business. She died of a heart attack in 1929. Her funeral was held at her house, the former Palace Manor, reportedly because no local churches wanted to perform services for a madam. Foozy died in 1934, and today their graves near the main road are enclosed with a fence made from plumber's pipes.

WOODPECKER HILL PRISON CEMETERY
Cañon City

This prison cemetery is part of Greenwood Cemetery, which is just west on CR 3 on the western edge of town, or at GPS 38.42720, -105.24640.

Colorado's prison inmates named this graveyard Woodpecker Hill because in the late 1800s, inmates' graves got only simple wooden markers—which hungry woodpeckers would destroy in their search for food.

This is where unclaimed prisoners' bodies were buried. Some six hundred graves are recorded here, but few have more than a cheap, prison-made marker. Woodpecker Hill is a depressing, tumbledown cemetery with a dark history, so ominous and final that the walk from a condemned man's cell to the Colorado gallows or gas chamber was called the "Woodpecker Waltz."

After the 1920s, the markers were made in the prison's license plate factory. They sometimes say only CSP INMATE.

Among the graves here are:

- **Joe Arridy** (1915–1939), a twenty-three-year-old retarded man wrongfully executed for bludgeoning two young girls with an ax. Arridy—who had the mental capacity of a five-year-old—confessed to witnessing the killing, and police were convinced they had already busted the real murderer in Pueblo with the murder weapon. Nevertheless, Arridy and the real killer, Frank Aguilar, were both convicted and sentenced to die. Prison officials and citizens fought to overturn Arridy's death sentence but failed. Arridy was executed in the gas chamber on January 6, 1939. Some seventy years later, a headstone was placed on his grave by some film producers who want to make a documentary about Arridy's case. Arridy was pardoned by the Colorado governor in 2011. His wrongful conviction is also explored in Robert Perske's

For over one hundred years, graves in Cañon City's desolate prison cemetery known as "Woodpecker Hill" have been marked only by small metal tags from the license plate shop.

1995 book *Deadly Innocence.* Look for a large marble headstone in Section 19 at GPS 38.42678, -105.24834.

- **Frank Aguilar** was executed on August 13, 1937. He is also buried at Woodpecker Hill, not far from Arridy at GPS 38.42670, -105.24834.

- **Luis Monge** (1918–1967) was the last man to die in Colorado's gas chamber and the last inmate in America to be executed before the U.S. Supreme Court outlawed capital punishment in 1972. He murdered his wife and three children in 1963 after his wife confronted him about an incestuous relationship he'd had with one of his daughters. He requested that when he died one of his corneas be transplanted to a juvenile delinquent; it was. As he was led into the gas chamber, Monge reportedly asked his executioner, "Will that gas bother my asthma?" Section 19 at GPS 38.42664, -105.24824.

- **John Freeze** (Inmate #9356) was doing life for murdering his wife. Newspapers called him "St. John the Baptist" because he was a preacher—and because he cut off his wife's head and brought it to the dinner table for his guests to see. He died of a ruptured appendix on July 9, 1943. His grave is marked by his name and number in Section 19 at GPS 38.42668, -105.24831.

- The **Pacheco brothers**—John, twenty-two, and Louis, thirty-seven—were condemned to die for killing two men. The brothers were so close that they asked the warden to allow them to be executed together. So on May 31, 1935, the Pacheco brothers sat together in the gas chamber and died. Their side-by-side graves are marked with their names and numbers—John #18012 and Louis #18013—in Section 19 at GPS 38.42640, -105.24834.

- **Edward Ives** (1884–1930) killed a Denver policeman and was sentenced to die by hanging. Weighing only eighty pounds, the diminutive Ives slipped through the noose when the gallows sprung. He jumped up and yelled, "You can't hang a man twice!" He was wrong. The second time worked. His grave is in the lower section's eastern first row with a small white stone marked with his name, at GPS 38.427558, -105.247977.

- **George Abshier** (d. 1930) was a member of the infamous Fleagle gang who was executed for his role in the deadly 1928 armed robbery of Lamar's First National Bank. Four innocent people were killed. Abshier and two other gang members—Howard Royston and Ralph Fleagle—were hanged over a two-week period in July 1930. His grave is marked simply CSP INMATE among hundreds just like it in the cemetery's lower section (GPS 38.42772, -105.248168). Nobody kept track of the anonymous burials.

See also Fleagle Gang Bank Robbery (Lamar).

MUSEUM OF COLORADO PRISONS
Cañon City

The museum is at 201 North First St., or GPS 38.43886, -105.24672. It sits beside the Colorado Territorial Correctional Facility, or "Old Max," an active prison. Summer hours are daily 8:30 a.m. to 6 p.m.; off-season hours are Wed–Sun 10–5. Admission charged; www.prisonmuseum.org.

Crime-and-punishment buffs will love this museum, which displays a weird assortment of items and exhibits, including the noose used in the last hanging execution in Colorado, the old Colorado gas chamber (outside in the fresh air of the courtyard), confiscated inmate weapons and other contraband, rare and historic photographs of prison life, disciplinary equipment used by guards since 1871, and a variety of prisoners' arts and crafts.

You may even sit in the cell of the famous Alfred Packer, the mountain-man cannibal who did time in Cañon City.

High-tech visitors can also rent MP3s and CDs for walking tours of the thirty-six "cells" where life-size models are displayed.

The museum is housed in the original Colorado Women's Prison, built in 1935 and used until 1968. Cañon City has been home to the Colorado State Penitentiary (East US 50 at GPS 38.440644, -105.157893) since the 1800s; today, more than a dozen other prison facilities are also based in Cañon City.

See also Cannibal Camp (Lake City).

ASSASSINATED JUDGE'S GRAVE
Castle Rock

Cedar Hill Cemetery is at 800 East Wolfensberger Rd. The grave is at GPS 39.37979, -104.87247.

In 1875, a water-rights squabble erupted into a full-scale war in the community of Granite. A brutal gang of vigilantes began to round up any troublemakers they could find. But when Judge Elias Foster Dyer (1836–1875) pressed charges against some of the vigilantes, he signed his own death warrant.

Dyer was murdered in his own courtroom by a mob, none of whom was ever arrested. While he waited to die, he wrote a note: "I trust in God and his mercy. At 8 o'clock I sit in court. The mob have me under guard. I die for law, order and principle."

His body was buried in a local Granite cemetery until relatives retrieved Dyer's body several years later and reburied him in a family plot in Castle Rock.

FEMALE SERIAL KILLER'S LAST VICTIM
Colorado Springs

Evergreen Cemetery is at 1005 Hancock Expressway. The grave is in Block 16, Lot 42, or GPS 38.81440, -104.79836.

German-born **Anna Marie Hahn** (1906–1938) was among America's relatively few documented female serial killers. If she hadn't been a rather clumsy thief, too, she might have gotten away with murder.

After a scandalous affair in Vienna, Austria, Anna Marie's parents sent her and her illegitimate son, Oskar, to America. They settled in Cincinnati, Ohio, where she soon married telegrapher Philip Hahn. After an argument, Philip got a dose of poison in his dinner, and while he survived, he never crossed his wife again.

By 1933, to support a growing gambling habit, Anna Marie began poisoning and robbing kindly old men in her neighborhood. The first was Ernst Kohler, whom she befriended just before his death. She convinced him to bequeath his house to her—then he died.

Over the next few years, Hahn killed eight people and tried to poison five others, almost always with arsenic mixed in their food. She then nursed them while she drained their bank accounts.

In 1937, Hahn met **Johan Obendoerfer,** a sixty-seven-year-old cobbler in Cincinnati. She told the infatuated old man that she owned a Colorado ranch where they could spend the rest of their lives together. So they made plans to travel to Colorado.

Along the way, Hahn put her murderous plan into action, sprinkling arsenic in Obendoerfer's food. By the time they reached Denver, he was quite ill, but they continued to Colorado Springs when hotel workers got too curious about the sick old man.

On July 30, 1937, Hahn, Oskar, and Obendoerfer arrived at the Denver & Rio Grande Railroad Depot (now a restaurant at 10 South Sierra Madre St., or GPS 38.833611, -104.828889), but Obendoerfer was so sick, he couldn't walk unaided to the Park Hotel across the street (it no longer exists but was in the area of the park across the street from the depot, GPS 38.833844, -104.828153).

Then Hahn made a fatal error. Seeing the innkeeper's private room unlocked, she stole two diamond rings. The innkeeper surprised Hahn coming out, although the theft was discovered much later.

Obendoerfer (1870–1937) died on August 1, but before he was buried as an indigent, Hahn and Oskar were racing out of town. In Denver she pawned the stolen rings for $7.50, then caught the next train to Ohio.

A week later, Cincinnati police questioned Hahn about the stolen rings—and, oh, the poor dead fellow she dumped in their town. Her stories didn't add up, and soon she was implicated in several murders.

Her monthlong trial was one of the most lurid of the 1930s. An autopsy found deadly levels of arsenic in Obendoerfer's body, so two of her other "friends" were also exhumed with the same result. She was convicted and sentenced to die in Ohio's electric chair, which she did on December 7, 1938. She maintained her innocence until the end, but a twenty-page handwritten confession was found after her death.

Anna Marie Hahn, the first female serial killer in the United States to die in the electric chair, is buried in Mount Calvary Cemetery in Columbus, Ohio.

See also Serial Child Killer's Victim (Colorado Springs).

MASS MURDER ... IN CHURCH
Colorado Springs
New Life Church is at 11025 Voyager Parkway, or GPS 38.991143, -104.796964.

On December 9, 2007, all Hell broke loose in a local megachurch.

That's when Matthew Murray, a twenty-four-year-old gunman armed with an assault rifle, two handguns, and more than one thousand rounds of ammunition, started shooting into a crowd of some seven thousand churchgoers leaving the crowded church.

The shootings followed an earlier bloodbath at Youth With a Mission, a missionary training school in Arvada where Murray had been expelled in 2004. Two people were killed at Youth With a Mission, 12750 West 64th Ave. in Arvada, or GPS 39.810591, -105.140957.

Raised in a deeply religious family, Murray was the home-schooled son of a prominent Denver neurologist. Police later said Murray "hated Christians." In Internet postings, Murray wrote that he would "rain Columbine down on the Christian world."

At New Life, Murray was wounded several times by a security officer, but he ultimately killed himself. In all, he'd killed four innocent people and wounded five others.

A memorial to two victims, sisters Rachel and Stephanie Works, is on the northeastern church grounds at GPS 38.99313, -104.79404.

Until 2006—just a year before the shootings—New Life Church was pastored by Rev. Ted Haggard, who was forced to resign after

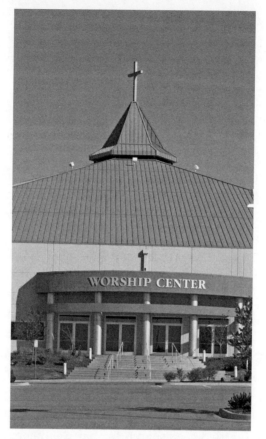

*Five people died when a deranged
young gunman opened fire at the New
Life Church and a missionary center
in 2007.*

admitting to "sexual immorality." A male prostitute claimed that
Haggard had paid him for sex and meth over a three-year period.
Murray later wrote that Christianity was, to him, only about "hate,
abuse (sexual, physical, psychological, and emotional), hypocrisy,
and lies."

Murray is buried in Denver's Fairmount Cemetery in Lot 97,
Block 116, at GPS 39.70217, -104.89782.

BOBBY BROWN BAIL BONDS
Colorado Springs

Bobby Brown's office is at 506 South Nevada Ave., or GPS 38.826506, -104.82237.

If you're a fan of A&E Network's *Dog the Bounty Hunter,* then you'll recognize Bobby Brown as the white-haired, mild-mannered bondsman who brings Duane "Dog" Chapman and his bounty-hunting family many of his cases. As a result of his association with Dog, former deputy and undercover cop Bobby Brown has become a celebrity on his own. His shop has a BEWARE OF DOG sign out front.

If you're just a suspect seeking bail, Bobby's number is 719-390-7031.

See also "Dog the Bounty Hunter" Childhood Home (Denver).

SERIAL CHILD KILLER'S VICTIM
Colorado Springs

Evergreen Cemetery is at 1005 North Hancock Ave. The grave is beside the road in Block 216, at GPS 38.81951, -104.79900.

Thirteen-year-old Heather Dawn Church (1978–1991) disappeared from her Black Forest home on September 17, 1991, launching a frustrating two-year search for her. Searchers finally found some of her bones in a remote area, and she was buried at Evergreen Cemetery.

Two years later, police arrested Robert Charles Browne, a Louisiana-born high school dropout who had been married six times (his wives were all still alive at the time of his arrest) and who had been kicked out of the U.S. Army for drug use. To avoid the death penalty, Browne eventually confessed to killing Church and another Colorado Springs child. He told his interrogators that none of his victims "ever got away ... never gave the opportunity."

He claims he has killed at least forty-eight people since 1970. He used knives, ice picks, or screwdrivers, then cut up some of his victims and dumped their corpses in lakes, rivers, dumpsters, and ditches.

In 2000, Browne sent investigators a mysterious, taunting letter. It included a traced map of Colorado and eight other states. The letter said: "Seven sacred virgins entombed side by side, those less worthy are scattered wide. The score is you 1, the other team 48."

Is he telling the truth? Browne, who is doing two life sentences without parole at a secret location, has reportedly given investigators specific details in nineteen murders and is a "strong suspect" in nine of them.

See also Female Serial Killer's Last Victim (Colorado Springs).

KILLING THE MAN WHO KILLED JESSE JAMES
Creede

The Old Creede Cemetery is just west of town off Bee McClure. Doctor Bob Ford's grave is a little north at GPS 37.85214, -106.93180.

"That dirty little coward" Robert Ford was gunned down in Creede, Colorado, in 1892, but his body was exhumed and reburied in Missouri.

In January 1882, an ambitious would-be outlaw named **Robert Ford** (1861–1892) killed a member of the James Gang. When he was arrested, he offered to deliver his friend Jesse James—dead or alive—in exchange for immunity (and a $10,000 reward).

Two months later, Robert Ford and his brother Charlie visited Jesse (then using the alias of Thomas Howard) at his St. Joseph, Missouri, home on the pretense of planning a bank robbery. But while Jesse straightened a picture on the wall, Robert Ford shot him once in the back of the head, killing him instantly.

Ford got his immunity and a small part of the $10,000 reward but was immediately scourged by locals who admired the James boys. He became known as "the dirty little coward who shot Mr. Howard." Embarrassed, he hit the road, starring in a poorly received stage show about the killing of Jesse James and lighting in various towns. Finally, he settled in Creede, Colorado, a wide-open boomtown where scoundrels like Soapy Smith and characters like Bat Masterson were already making headlines and profits.

A crime boss, Smith owned the Orleans Exchange on Main Street, and Masterson managed the Denver Exchange a few doors down. So on May 29, 1892, Ford opened Ford's Exchange on Main Street. Unfortunately, Creede's entire downtown district burned to the ground six days later, but the day after the fire Ford quickly set up a new tent saloon at approximately GPS 37.85147, -106.92696 (now a market's parking lot). The devastating fire leveled Creede, and today the exact sites are more a matter of oral history than documentation.

Ford's business was short-lived. The day after he opened, a thug named **Ed O'Kelley** (1858–1904) walked into the bar and greeted Ford, whose back was to the door. As Ford turned, O'Kelley blasted him with both barrels of his sawed-off shotgun. Ford was originally buried in the Old Creede Cemetery but was later exhumed and reburied in his hometown of Richmond, Missouri. His empty Creede grave is now marked for the sake of tourists.

O'Kelley served ten years in prison for killing the man who killed Jesse James. Two years after his 1902 release, O'Kelley was killed by cops in Oklahoma City, where he is now buried in Fairlawn Cemetery.

Although he'd made a name for himself in Colorado in crime, **Soapy Smith** (1860–1898) went to the Yukon to strike it rich off miners' dreams and died in a shootout with vigilantes. He is buried in the City Cemetery in Skagway, Alaska.

Legendary ex-lawman **Bat Masterson** (1853–1921) went on to become a prizefight promoter and popular newspaper columnist in New York. He died at his desk of a heart attack and is buried in Woodlawn Cemetery in the Bronx, New York.

CHER ELDER'S CLANDESTINE GRAVESITE
West of Empire

This primitive memorial is at GPS 39.76331, -105.72086. To get there, drive west from the Colorado town of Empire about two miles on US 40 to a highway turnout on the north side of the highway, where you'll see a rather prominent National Forest sign (GPS 39.762815, -105.719971). Walk up the adjacent hill to a footpath that will take you northwesterly. Within fifty yards, you'll reach a small glade with a large pile of rocks and a permanent marker where visitors often leave memorial items.

In March 1993, Cher Elder had an argument with her boyfriend. Soon after, the twenty-year-old from Golden, Colorado, was seen leaving a Central City casino with Tom Luther, a convicted rapist recently freed after eleven years in prison. In fact, Luther was still a suspect in the 1982 murders of two other women. In prison, he'd told a friend that his next victim would die and police would never find her body.

The "next" victim was Cher Elder, who was not seen alive again. Luther shot her three times in the back of her head, then cut off her ring finger and lips because she threatened to expose an illegal sports-card ring connected to him.

Cher's body was found in 1995 in a hidden grave not far from I-70 in the forest west of Empire. Luther had fled to West Virginia, where he raped and beat a hitchhiker in 1994. He was caught and convicted for that attack and then returned to Colorado, where he was convicted of Elder's slaying too. He was sentenced to forty-eight years in Elder's murder and will begin serving his time after he gets out of prison in West Virginia. He remains a suspect in at least eight other murders and rapes.

Investigators believe Luther used the National Forest sign as a "marker" for where he'd buried his victim under a pile of rocks so he could return.

Cher Elder (1973–1993) was properly reburied in Lot 210 of Grand Junction's Orchard Mesa Cemetery (IOOF Section) at GPS 39.04401, -108.56868.

The case is explored in Steve Jackson's 1998 book *Monster*.

SAMSON'S MOUNTED HEAD
Estes Park
The YMCA of the Rockies is at 2515 Tunnel Rd., or GPS 40.34039, -105.57159.

In the 1990s, an enormous bull elk named Samson became Estes Park's unofficial mascot. Gentle and majestic with his eight-by-nine-point rack, he wandered the open spaces around the local YMCA camp like a photo op on the hoof.

In 1995, the laziest poacher in the world killed Samson with a single arrow from a crossbow. The dope spent ninety days in jail, lost hunting privileges for life (and his driver's license for two years), and paid more than $8,000 in fines and court costs.

The entire town grieved Samson's murder. His head was mounted and now hangs above the massive stone fireplace left of

In 1995, a poacher killed Samson, a familiar bull elk, and Estes Park memorialized the animal in taxidermy, bronze ... and beer.

the main door in the administrative building of the YMCA of the Rockies. This gentle giant was also memorialized with a statue at the intersection of US 36 and CO 7 at the east entrance to Estes Park (GPS 40.37561, -105.50938). As if that were not enough, a local beer has also been named in his honor: Samson's Stout.

THE SHINING HOTEL
Estes Park

The Stanley Hotel is at 333 Wonderview Ave., or GPS 40.3825, -105.519167

Sure, it was built by the inventor of the Stanley Steamer automobile. Sure, it's a 138-room Georgian hotel with an unparalleled view of the Rockies. Sure, it's more than one hundred years old.

But the Stanley's biggest claim to fame is as the inspiration for Stephen King's chilling masterwork *The Shining.* You can actually stay in Room 217, where King wrote much of the book. In the book, much of the action takes place in Room 217 of the fictional Overlook Hotel; the movie version changed it to 237.

Stanley Kubrick's film version of *The Shining* wasn't filmed at the Stanley. Jack Nicholson's Overlook Hotel was just an English film set, although a few exterior shots were from the Timberline Lodge in Mount Hood, Oregon.

ADX FLORENCE, OR "SUPERMAX" PRISON
Florence

Unless you commit an especially heinous federal crime, you won't get close enough to Supermax for a vacation photo, but it's at GPS 38.356389, -105.094444.

Built into a mountainside, Supermax prison is known as the "Alcatraz of the Rockies," a thirty-seven-acre complex festooned with motion detectors, 1,400 remote-controlled steel doors, laser beams, barbed-wire fences, pressure pads, and attack dogs, where no single serious escape attempt has ever been made since it was built in 1994.

Among the more than four hundred prisoners there at any time are the worst of the worst in the federal system, from terrorists to serial killers to drug lords.

Most of the prisoners are held in solitary confinement for twenty-three hours every day. They live in soundproof seven-by-twelve-foot cells with only a sliver of light. For one hour each day they are allowed to exercise in a concrete chamber, wearing shackles.

Prisoners seldom see each other. Their only real human contact is with guards or other staffers. Most of the furniture in their cells—except for the metal toilets—is poured concrete. They are separated from tightly screened visitors by glass, and religious services are broadcast from a small chapel.

Some former prisoners have called it a "living tomb"; a former warden calls it "a cleaner version of Hell."

Among Supermax's current and former guests are 9/11 conspirator Zacarias Moussaoui; shoe bomber Richard Reid; Unabomber Ted Kaczynski; Oklahoma City bomber Terry Nichols (and until his execution, Timothy McVeigh); racist murderer H. Rap Brown; former FBI spy Robert Hanssen; mob hit man Sammy "The Bull" Gravano; ex-Enron schemer Andrew Fastow, who lives in a minimum security camp within Supermax; hit man Charles Harrelson, the late father of actor Woody Harrelson; Mexican Mafia godfather Raul Leon; Olympic Park bomber Eric Rudolph; and mobster James Sabatino, who might (or might not) have killed rapper Tupac Shakur.

White supremacist David Lane, convicted as the wheelman in the 1984 murder of Denver talk-radio host Alan Berg, died at Supermax in 2007.

See also Alan Berg's Murder Scene (Denver).

THE BLOODY ESPINOSAS
Fort Garland

The Fort Garland Museum is on the site of the original frontier fort at 29477 CO 159, or GPS 37.423889, -105.432222. Summer hours daily 9-5; off-season Thu-Mon 8-4. Admission charged; www.museumtrail.org/fortgarlandmuseum.asp.

Serial killers have been around almost as long as humans have stood upright, even though our fascination with them didn't really begin until Jack the Ripper's slaughter in 1888 London. The term "serial killer" didn't even enter our lexicon until 1973.

But in the 1860s, two angry Mexican brothers named Felipe and Juan Espinosa claimed in a letter to the Colorado territorial governor to have been commanded by the Virgin Mary to go out and kill one hundred "gringos" for each of their six relatives killed in the Mexican War.

And soon, they were making good on their mission.

At least thirty-two people were killed, most of them ambushed in the Leadville and California Gulch area (GPS 39.224167, -106349167). The butchered remains of one of the Espinosas' victims, teamster **Henry Harkins**, are buried in Dead Man's Canyon in El Paso County. His headstone is on the southeast side of CO 115 about one mile south of Fort Carson's main entrance, or GPS 38.67117, -104.85839.

Marshals and soldiers weren't enough to end the Espinosas' killing spree. The governor called upon legendary trapper and scout **Tom Tobin** (1823–1904) to bring them in, dead or alive.

For days, Tobin tracked the Espinosas to a remote camp, where he killed Felipe and a cousin (Juan was already dead) then returned to Fort Garland.

Back at Fort Garland, the commandant asked Tobin if he'd had any luck. Tobin emptied a gunnysack containing the severed heads of Felipe and his cousin on the floor (the fort's commandant's quarters are at GPS 37.424323, -105.432283).

It's said that Felipe Espinosa's head was kept for a time in the basement of the Colorado Capitol, then later it was pickled in a jar and traveled the sideshow circuit for many years. However, its whereabouts today are unknown.

Tobin only got a small part of the $2,500 reward offered. He died in 1904 and was buried in a now-abandoned ranch cemetery near Fort Garland. His elaborate stone, which misspells his name, is now in the MacMullen Cemetery (GPS 37.436706, -105.464646) on private land owned by the Trinchera Ranch. Permission is necessary to visit.

TRANSGENDER MURDER VICTIM'S GRAVE
Fort Lupton

Hillside Cemetery is at 13750 Weld CR 12, just southwest of town. The grave is at GPS 40.07245, -104.79436.

Born a male, Justin Zapata wanted to be a woman. He soon began identifying himself as Angie, wore makeup and long hair, behaved like a woman, and even had a dream of winning the Miss Latina beauty pageant. But on July 17, 2008, eighteen-year-old Angie was murdered in her Greeley apartment by a young man she had just met two days before. Prosecutors argued the new boyfriend—Allen Andrade, thirty-two—was a homophobe who beat Angie to death when he discovered she was a he (Angie remained biologically a male). Andrade was convicted and is serving a life sentence without the possibility of parole.

MILLIONAIRE'S HIT-AND-RUN VICTIM
Golden

Golden Cemetery is at 755 Ulysses St. The grave is in Block 247B, Lot 2 of the City Section, or GPS 39.73016, -105.19659.

Rocky Mountain News columnist **Greg Lopez** (1961–1996) was killed one night when a rare BMW 540i going more than 100 mph rear-ended his SUV on I-25. Lopez was not only a popular voice in Denver media— he had recently learned his wife was pregnant.

The BMW was traced to Spicer Breeden, a thirty-six-year-old heir to the Boettcher fortune. Breeden loved fast cars almost as much as he loved cocaine. Breeden had never worked a day in his life. The quintessential spoiled rich brat, he inherited millions at age thirteen and grew up in a Boettcher family mansion atop Lookout Mountain. His cocaine addiction made him irrationally paranoid: He sprinkled cornflakes on his floors to warn him of intruders, and he believed the FBI was tunneling under his house and watching him through his TV.

After an afternoon of drinking and drugs on March 17, 1996, Breeden and a friend hopped in his "cosmos black" BMW and sped toward Denver. Speeding at more than 100 mph while weaving through traffic, their car smashed into Lopez's vehicle, which barrel-rolled four times and killed him, even though he was wearing a seatbelt.

Witnesses saw Breeden's car stop briefly, then drive off. In fact, Breeden and his friend went home to switch cars, then returned to bar-hopping in Denver's chic LoDo district.

Two days later, police traced Breeden's car. As they knocked on his door, he pushed furniture against the doors and windows and watched TV coverage while he drank and snorted himself into a haze.

Then he went into his bathroom, where he first wounded his dog then killed himself. In a hastily scrawled will, he left his last $500,000 to his girlfriend and claimed he wasn't driving the BMW that killed Lopez, but a year later a jury acquitted his companion in the death.

Spicer Breeden (1960–1996) was cremated and his ashes were scattered around the Boettcher Mansion on Lookout Mountain (GPS 39.73033, -105.24915. (This is private property.)

Also in the Golden Cemetery:

- **Matthaeus Jaehnig** (1972–1997) was not just the scion of a wealthy family—his father founded Denver's Waldorf School, which teaches racial tolerance—but he was a radical skinhead too. On November 6, 1997, this privileged high-school dropout led police on a high-speed chase. While his girlfriend drove, he fired at his pursuers with an automatic rifle. Finally cornered, Jaehnig killed Officer Bruce Vanderjagt, then committed suicide with the cop's gun. Jaehnig was buried in Block 268, Lot 4 in the City Section, or GPS 39.72924, -105.19710. A former Marine, Vanderjagt was buried in the Fort Rosecrans National Cemetery in San Diego, California.

- Although the story is now disputed, Columbine victim **Cassie Bernall** (1981–1999) was reportedly cowering under a desk when she was asked by teenage mass-murderer Eric

Harris if she believed in God. She said yes, and he shot her dead. In one eyewitness account, Harris simply slapped his hand on the desk and bent over to say, "Peekaboo!" before killing Cassie. Her mother, Misty Bernall, later wrote one of several books about the Columbine tragedy, *She Said Yes: The Unlikely Martyrdom of Cassie Bernall.* Her grave is in the City section, just south of the intersection of the Frontier and Pathfinder Paths, or GPS 39.73057, -105.19563.

See also Mass Murder at Columbine (Littleton).

A VAMPIRE'S GRAVE?
Lafayette

Lafayette Municipal Cemetery is on the northern edge of Lafayette, just north of CO 7/Baseline Road, a half mile east of US 287. The grave is in the pauper's section in the northwestern part of the graveyard, although it is marked at GPS 40.00145, -105.09272.

Just because a guy is from Transylvania doesn't mean he is a vampire ... does it?

Fodor Glava was born in the same mysterious region as Bram Stoker's fictional Count Dracula (and his real-life inspiration, a cruel king named Vlad the Impaler). He immigrated to America in the late 1880s and became a coal miner. He even enlisted as a soldier in World War I but died in the 1918 influenza epidemic. But before he died, Glava bought a grave plot in the Lafayette cemetery's pauper's field, in which he was buried with another flu victim, James Trandofir—a common practice at the time. And that's where the legend of Fodor Glava takes a weird turn.

Even then, some people were whispering that Glava might be a vampire. Local gossip said somebody hammered a wooden stake through his heart after he died ... just to be sure.

Today a tree grows out of the grave at about the same spot where Glava's heart would be. Did the wooden stake take root in the vampire's heart?

Some visitors to the grave aren't taking any chances. If you visit, you might see salt sprinkled around the headstone. This is a traditional ritual to keep the "evil spirit" from escaping the grave.

FLEAGLE GANG BANK ROBBERY
Lamar

The former First National Bank was at 122 South Main, or GPS 38.08832, -102.61935.

The Fleagle Gang wasn't the best-known gaggle of bank robbers and killers of the gangster era, but they made crime history when their robbery of the First National Bank became the first case to turn on the discovery of a single fingerprint. It was also the first time airplanes were used to track a getaway car from the scene of the crime.

Over ten-plus years, brothers Jake and Ralph Fleagle (and cohorts) stole at least $1 million—and maybe much more—from banks and trains in Colorado, Kansas, Oregon, and California.

Early on May 23, 1928, four gun-wielding robbers—the Fleagles, George Abshier, and Heavy Royston—entered the First National Bank. As they stuffed money into pillowcases, bank president A. N. Parrish snatched a gun from his desk and fired—wounding Royston. The robbers shot Parrish dead, and when his son John Parrish rushed to his side, they shot him too.

Taking two hostages—one-armed Edward Lundgren and Everett Kesinger—the robbers fled in their blue 1927 Buick Master Six with more than $220,000 in cash, bonds, and commercial paper.

Back home in Kansas, the Fleagles killed hostage Kesinger and released Lundgren. They also killed a country doctor who treated

Gangster Jake Fleagle
FBI

Royston's wound, then hid the doctor's car—which bore a single fingerprint left on the windshield by Jake Fleagle.

The fledgling FBI matched the fingerprint to Jake, who was subsequently killed in Branson, Missouri. The rest were arrested, convicted, and executed by hanging at the Colorado State Penitentiary in Cañon City in July 1930. The Fleagle brothers are buried in Garden City, Kansas; Royston is buried in Richmond, California; and Abshier is buried at Woodpecker Hill Prison Cemetery in Cañon City.

A. N. and John Parrish, the father-and-son bankers killed in the robbery, are buried at Fairmount Cemetery on Memorial Drive about a mile south of town; their graves are in Plot 71 at GPS 38.05119,

-102.60783. Slain hostage Kesinger (1901-1928) is buried near them at Fairmount in Block 3, Lot 21, or GPS 38.05107, -102.60790.

The Big Timbers Museum, 7515 West US 50 in Lamar (GPS 38.115849, -102.618806), displays five guns used in the robbery, the original fingerprint cards, the Fleagles' getaway car, and some furniture from the bank. The museum is open in summer, daily hours 10–5; winter hours 1–4. Admission charged; www .bigtimbersmuseum.com.

Grand Junction's Museum of Western Colorado displays a shotgun used in the holdup.

The window from one of the gang's getaway cars—with the original fingerprint—was displayed at the Federal Bureau of Investigation in Washington, D.C., for more than twenty years but was eventually stored and lost. The window was later found and now is at the Finney County Museum in Kansas.

The robbery is detailed in N. T. Betz's 2005 book *The Fleagle Gang: Betrayed by a Fingerprint.*

Also see Cannibal Camp (Lake City); Woodpecker Hill Prison Cemetery in Cañon City.

CLAY ALLISON VICTIM'S GRAVE
Las Animas

Las Animas Cemetery is about a mile south of town at the intersection of CR 10.75 and CR EE, or GPS 38.04250, -103.21750. The grave location is unmarked and unknown but is believed to be in the oldest section.

Gunslinger **Clay Allison** (1840–1877) was one of the Old West's most psychotic gunslingers. In his short career, his body count was at least fifteen men.

One of them was Deputy **Charlie Faber**, who'd been called to quell a disturbance at Las Animas's rowdy Olympic Dance Hall (believed to have been on the west side of Carson Street, between 4th and 5th Streets, or GPS 38.068253, -103.221467) on December 21, 1876. In the melee, Faber was fatally shot by Allison. Allison was charged with manslaughter, but when no eyewitnesses appeared, he was freed.

Faber's grave has been lost, but he is honored on Panel 29, W-20, on the National Law Enforcement Officers Memorial in Washington, D.C.

Allison died the next year, not in a gunfight but by falling off a freight wagon he was driving. His neck was crushed by a wheel. He later died from his injuries and was buried in Pecos, Texas.

AN UNLIKELY STAGE ROBBER
Balltown (Leadville area)

The lone gravesite is near Balltown at the junction of US 24 and CO 82, just fifteen miles south of Leadville. A half mile north of the junction, it can be seen on a hillside across the railroad tracks and creek from US 24 at GPS 39.082884, -106.282862

In the last 1870s, gold shipments from Leadville were a closely guarded secret, but the stagecoach was being robbed with uncanny regularity when the gold was aboard. Lawmen suspected an inside job, so they contrived a "sting" operation to catch the robber.

Sure enough, the stagecoach carrying the fake gold shipment was stopped by a masked robber near Balltown, but deputies quickly shot the highwayman dead.

When the robber's mask was removed, one of the deputies was horrified to recognize his wife. Too ashamed to take her back to Leadville, he buried her on the spot beside the wagon road. He erected a headstone still visible (to sharp eyes) from US 24. It reads: MY WIFE—JANE KIRKHAM—DIED MARCH 7, 1879—AGED 38 YEARS, 3 MONTHS, 7 DAYS.

BUFFALO BILL'S GRAVE
Lookout Mountain

The gravesite and museum is at 987½ Lookout Mountain Rd., just off I-70 west of Golden. GPS 39.73257, -105.23824.

The legendary William F. Cody (1846–1917), better known as Buffalo Bill, was not a lawman, outlaw, or even a victim. So why is he included in a book about crime-related sites in Colorado? Well, he was almost stolen goods—or maybe he was.

The former Union scout, buffalo hunter, and Indian fighter helped define the frontier with his famous Wild West show. He founded the town of Cody, Wyoming, where he eventually settled. Without a doubt, he was the biggest celebrity of his day.

On January 10, 1917, Buffalo Bill died at age seventy while visiting his sister's Denver home (2932 Lafayette St., or GPS 39.758928, -104.97080). An enormous controversy erupted: Should Buffalo Bill be buried in his beloved Cody, where he had reportedly picked out a gravesite … or in Colorado, where his wife wanted to bury him?

More than twenty thousand mourners paid their respects as Buffalo Bill lay in state at Colorado's Capitol rotunda (200 East Colfax in Denver, GPS 39.739236, -104.984858).

But rumors began to circulate that some angry cowboys from Cody (and a few relatives) were planning to steal Buffalo Bill's corpse and bring it back to Wyoming. Security was beefed up around Cody's body, which was kept on ice until it could be buried six months later at an elaborate ceremony on Lookout Mountain, just west of Denver.

As an extra precaution, the undertakers asked his widow, Louisa, to identify the body one last time before it was lowered into the steel-reinforced vault. He was then buried beneath ten tons of concrete—to dissuade body-snatchers—on Lookout Mountain. Just in case, the Colorado National Guard parked an armored tank nearby.

Colorado originally had plans for an elaborate monument over the grave, but it never happened. It remains a simple site surrounded

*Fearing grave-robbers who believed
Buffalo Bill wanted a Wyoming funeral,
law enforcement tightened security after
the showman was buried.*

by a wrought-iron fence. Today a souvenir shop, refreshment bar, and a museum stand nearby.

But some folks believe Buffalo Bill's corpse really was snatched before it was buried and now lies in a secret grave on Cedar Mountain (GPS 44.4932, -109.1697) overlooking Cody, Wyoming.

One thing is certain: The mystery will never be solved without a lot of hard digging and hiking.

ADOLPH COORS III KIDNAPPING AND MURDER
Morrison area

Turkey Creek Bridge no longer exists but was replaced by the newer US 285/CO 470 interchange at the site.

Early on February 9, 1960, Adolph Coors III left his country home in the foothills of the Rockies to go to work as chairman of his family's brewery in Golden. And that was the last anyone saw the forty-four-year-old beer executive alive—except his killer.

Coors's car was later found running on the Turkey Creek Bridge. Investigators found his hat and eyeglasses in the creek below and blood spatters on the bridge.

The next day, Coors's wife, Mary, received a ransom note asking for $500,000 and telling her to place a tractor ad in the *Denver Post* to signal when she had the money. She placed the ad, but the kidnapper never responded.

Police were already looking for a man named Walter Osborne, whose canary yellow 1951 Mercury had been seen in the area even

Killer Joe Corbett
FBI

The corpse of beer executive Joseph Coors III was found in this remote mountain dump seven months after he disappeared.

though he lived in a one-bedroom downtown Denver apartment (1435 Pearl St., #305, or GPS 39.739216, -104.980041). The day of the kidnapping, Osborne had moved out in a hurry.

Despite a nationwide manhunt, the trail was cold until Osborne's yellow car was found burned in Atlantic City, New Jersey, and dirt from its wheel wells tied it to the murder scene. Suddenly Walter Osborne—who was really an escaped California murderer named Joseph Corbett—was added to the FBI's Ten Most Wanted list.

But Corbett, an unlikely killer, was in the wind. Born in Seattle, he was a Fulbright Scholar at the University of Oregon with a genius IQ who'd killed a hitchhiker in California in 1950. He was sent to prison for five years to life but escaped four years later. He landed in Denver as Walter Osborne and worked at a paint factory.

Obsessed with the Lindbergh baby kidnapping, Corbett planned to kidnap the wealthy Adolph Coors III. He mail-ordered pistols, leg irons, a Royalite typewriter, handcuffs, and the yellow Mercury to do it.

In September—almost eight months after Coors's disappearance—his decomposing skeleton was found in a mountain dump eight miles southwest of Sedalia, Colorado (GPS 39.33157, -105.04803). He'd been shot twice in the back. Visit this site and you'll wonder how police ever found the body.

Six weeks later, the FBI arrested Corbett in Vancouver, British Columbia. In 1961, he was convicted of murder and sentenced to life in prison.

Corbett was paroled at age fifty-two in 1980. He moved into a small apartment at 2801 South Federal Blvd., #307, or GPS 39.664851, -105.025349. The two-time killer lived there quietly and drove a Salvation Army truck until August 24, 2009, when he shot himself in the head. Nobody claimed his body, and he was buried at Mount Olivet Cemetery, 12801 West 44th Ave. in Wheat Ridge. His unmarked grave is at GPS 39.78223, -105.14192 (beside a stone for "Kusner").

Adolph Coors III (1915-1960) was cremated and his ashes spread over Aspen Mountain (GPS 39.176099, -106.829206). Oddly, his father, Adolph Coors II, had also been the target of an abortive kidnapping in 1934 when two Prohibition agents conspired to ransom him for $50,000. The plot was broken up before it happened.

EMILY GRIFFITH MURDER
Pinecliffe

The murder cabin is literally inside a modern home at GPS 39.931725, -105.429649. The suspected killer's cabin still exists a mile west at GPS 39.93817, -105.44313.

Emily Griffith (1868–1947) was truly one of the pioneers of American education. In 1916, she established the Opportunity School, America's first public school to offer vocational training to anyone who wanted it, regardless of age, gender, or race. It opened in a condemned school building at 13th and Welton Streets in Denver (GPS 39.741174, -104.995437). The school has evolved over the past century into a sprawling vocational/technical college on the same site, although the original building is long gone.

In 1927, Griffith and her sister Florence also founded #9 Pearl St., a home for homeless boys (no longer existent).

Upon retiring, Emily and **Florence** (1881–1947) moved to a small cabin in Pinecliffe, a tiny town in the mountains southeast of Nederland in Gilpin County. The cabin itself was built by **Fred Lundy,** a former teacher at the Opportunity School and a dear friend who lived in a similar cabin nearby.

On June 19, 1947, the elderly sisters were both found shot in the back of the head in their cabin. Since they had little money and few possessions, robbery was ruled out. Instead, suspicion fixed on Lundy, who had reportedly told someone he would "rather see [Emily and Florence] dead than the way they were living." Newspapers quickly concluded it had been a mercy killing—and Lundy disappeared.

Searchers found Lundy's hat beneath a railroad bridge over nearby South Boulder Creek (GPS 39.937299, -105.438184). His empty

Former teacher Fred Lundy, who lived in this mountain cabin, helped the Griffith sisters build a cabin nearby—and might have killed them too.

Educator Emily Griffith

1941 Nash sedan was parked on the road containing what appeared to be a suicide note, but there was no sign of Lundy.

The Griffith sisters were buried together during a grand funeral at Denver's Fairmount Cemetery, 430 South Quebec St. Their graves are in Lot 27, Block 61, at GPS 39.71014, -104.90068.

Two months later, Lundy's body was fished out of South Boulder Creek, without any signs of foul play. Authorities ruled Lundy had killed the Griffith sisters and committed suicide by drowning himself in the creek. Lundy was cremated and his ashes reportedly sent home to Illinois. The case was closed.

But in her 2005 Griffith biography, *Touching Tomorrow,* Colorado author-historian Debra Faulkner suggests a new suspect: the Griffiths' surviving sister and brother-in-law, Ethel and Evans Gurtner, who inherited the women's modest estates. Evans was a known shady character who might have been deeply in debt to unsavory creditors.

After the murder, the Gurtners spent much of their time cruising the world's seas until Ethel died unexpectedly in 1949. Evans buried her beside her sisters, but he never placed a headstone there, and soon he remarried to a wife who also died unexpectedly a few years later.

A site you WON'T find in Pueblo!
The Black Dahlia's fiancé

The gruesome 1947 murder of Elizabeth Short—better known as the Black Dahlia—is one of the most intriguing unsolved American crimes of the twentieth century. And it has a connection to Pueblo, Colorado—although you can't visit any sites here.

Short was a twenty-two-year-old would-be actress who mostly supported herself by dalliances with men she met and seduced. On January 15, 1947, Short's mutilated nude body was discovered in a vacant lot near Hollywood. It had been cut in half at the waist and drained of blood. Her killer also sliced open her mouth from ear to ear and posed her body in a grotesque position.

The murder has never been solved, although many theories have been proposed over the years.

But during World War II, Short had met Major Matthew Michael Gordon Jr., a heroic Army Air Corps pilot from Pueblo who was soon deployed to Burma. Short told friends that Gordon had proposed to her in a letter while recovering from a crash in India and that she had accepted. Unfortunately, Gordon was killed in another crash in India on August 10, 1945—five days before the war ended—and never made it home to marry Short. His Army buddies confirmed his relationship with Short, but for many years, his family didn't believe it. It didn't help that Short later embellished the story to suggest a clandestine marriage to Gordon had produced a child that died too.

Short was buried at Mountain View Cemetery in Oakland, California. A copy of Gordon's obituary was found in her purse after her murder. Her case remains open.

Gordon never made it home, even in death. He was buried at the National Memorial Cemetery of the Pacific in Honolulu, Hawaii.

MOB BOSS'S GRAVE
Pueblo

Roselawn Cemetery is at 1706 Roselawn Rd. Crypt 13EE is in Mausoleum 1, or GPS 38.24142, -104.57831.

Handsome **Joseph "Scotty" Spinuzzi** (1908–1975) started his criminal career as a small-time counterfeiter, bootlegger, and safecracker, but he rose through the gangland ranks to become boss of the Colorado Family when James Colletti retired in 1969. In 1971, Spinuzzi went to prison for a year on gambling charges. He died of natural causes in 1975, and the Smaldone Brothers assumed control of the syndicate.

See also Denver's Brother Hoods (Denver).

SAND CREEK MASSACRE OF 1864
Sand Creek

The battlefield and monument—now a National Historic Site—are in southeastern Colorado. Enter the park from CO 96 at CR 54 or 59. Drive north to Kiowa CR W and follow the signs to the headquarters at GPS 38.544699, -102.503858. The park is open daily 9–4 in summer; check with the park for winter hours. Free admission; www.nps.gov/sand.

In 1851, the U.S. government officially recognized that Cheyenne and Arapaho tribes owned a vast parcel of land that enveloped what is today southeastern Wyoming, southwestern Nebraska, western Kansas, and almost all of Colorado's eastern plains. But in 1858, gold was discovered in Colorado, unleashing a deluge of white miners, settlers, shopkeepers, and other adventurers across that Indian land.

So in 1861, the government renegotiated with the Arapaho and Cheyenne tribes. Six chiefs, including the Southern Cheyenne's Black Kettle, accepted a new, much smaller reservation, angering militant warriors known as Dog Soldiers, who continued to live and hunt on the old lands—and make trouble for white immigrants.

The hostility simmered until 1864, when white politicians in Colorado had grown impatient with the Indians. To protect his people, Black Kettle negotiated new peace accords and was told to camp near Fort Lyon along Sand Creek, where they would be safe.

So Black Kettle and about 800 followers set up camp at Sand Creek, where they sent warriors to hunt. Black Kettle even flew an American flag to show his tribe's friendliness.

On the morning of November 29, 1864, Colonel John Chivington—with the blessing of Governor John Evans—ordered seven

Colonel John Chivington

hundred of his Colorado Cavalry troops to attack Black Kettle's village. Two officers—Captain Silas Soule and Lieutenant Joseph Cramer—refused, but the rest of Chivington's men struck with muskets and cannons.

The running assault ranged over five miles from the camp as Indians fled northward under a white flag. In the end, the camp was wiped out, although Black Kettle survived. The actual number of Indian dead is unknown; Chivington claimed it was as many as six hundred, but later historians estimated it to be 70 to 163, mostly women and children. Some twenty-four soldiers died, and it has been suggested that they were mostly victims of friendly fire by their hungover comrades.

Chivington's men declared a great victory and scavenged many war trophies from the camp, including scalps, ears, fetuses, and genitals of dead Indians, which they displayed with great pride back in Denver.

Ghostly, windswept plains surround a simple marker on the site of the 1864 Sand Creek massacre, where an untold number of innocent Indians were killed.

Captain Silas Soule refused to follow orders to fire on a peaceful Indian camp at Sand Creek—and was mysteriously murdered less than a year later.

An official investigation was launched against Chivington and his officers, but no charges were ever brought. The government apologized for the killings and promised reparation, but no money was ever paid.

Governor **John Evans** (1814–1897), who approved the attack, lost his territorial governorship and became a champion of western railroads. He is buried at Denver's Riverside Cemetery in Section 13, or GPS 39.79390, -104.96156.

Colonel **John M. Chivington** (1821–1894) is buried at Denver's Fairmount Cemetery. His grave is in Lot 143, Block 2, or at GPS 39.70853, -104.89995. **Harper Orahood** (1841–1915), one of Chivington's willing officers, is also in Fairmount in Lot 113/114, Block 15, at GPS 39.70676, -104.89869.

Captain **Silas Soule** (1838–1865), son of abolitionists, is one of the unsung heroes of the massacre. By refusing to participate in the slaughter and later testifying against Chivington, he stood on principle at a difficult moment. In 1865, Soule became a marshal in Denver and was assassinated a few days later by a soldier who had ties to Chivington; the killer was never tried. Soule is buried in Denver's Riverside Cemetery in Lot 4, Block 27, at GPS 39.79340, -104.95774.

The massacre touched off a more intense war between militant Dog Soldiers and whites that continued through bloody battles at the Washita, Little Big Horn, and Wounded Knee.

The 13,000-acre Sand Creek Massacre National Historic Site was dedicated in 2007, 142 years after the attack. A memorial stone has been erected at GPS 38.54954, -102.51151.

The Sand Creek Massacre is depicted in two 1970 Hollywood films, *Soldier Blue* and *Little Big Man*. It is also explored in Jerome Greene and Douglas Scott's 2007 history, *Finding Sand Creek*.

HIGH-PLAINS SERIAL KILLERS
Stratton

The site of the clandestine burials is on a private ranch at 13421 CR 29, or GPS 39.235093, -102.63285. This is private property.

A father and son who might be Colorado's most prolific serial killers might have dodged justice—but neither eluded death.

In February 1986, Michael McCormick led homicide detectives to the secret graves of three men buried on his father's 2,800-acre ranch south of the small, eastern plains town of Stratton. McCormick, who'd been arrested for stealing a missing trucker's rig, claimed his father killed the man and buried him in a wheat field.

But that wasn't all. McCormick claimed his father, Tom McCormick, also picked up as many as seventeen homeless men at a Denver shelter, made them work on the ranch (or recruited them to his car-theft ring), then killed them rather than paying them. Mike led investigators to three shallow graves, but before he could show them the rest, the investigation ran out of money.

With only flimsy evidence from a confessed conspirator, prosecutors refused to charge Tom with murder. Instead, they only charged Mike, who was convicted of first-degree murder in 1987. When an appeals court overturned his conviction, Mike cut a deal that let him get out of prison in 2005 instead of facing a retrial.

Even today, investigators and volunteers occasionally search for old graves they believe remain on the former McCormick Ranch, but none has ever been found.

The suspected killers will be no help. Never charged in the crime, **Tom McCormick** (1933-1997) died in Aurora of natural causes and is buried in the Flagler Cemetery, about one and a half miles east of Flagler, Colorado, on CR U. The grave is at GPS 39.28869, -103.03565.

In 2010, fifty-three-year-old **Mike McCormick** killed himself in a murder-suicide at 109 Timber Court in Granby (GPS 40.046695, -105.89977). He had abducted his business partner, who'd rebuffed his romantic overtures, and then killed her before shooting himself.

LUDLOW MASSACRE
Trinidad area
The massacre site and memorial is about thirteen miles north of Trinidad. Take exit 27 off I-25 and drive about a mile west on CR 44. The site is at GPS 37.339256, -104.58388.

A visitor center on the site of the Ludlow camp near Trinidad memorializes the twenty five dead—mostly women and children—in the strike-breaking attack.

Colorado's gold, silver, and coal riches tapped into the mother lode of men's dreams … and took them deep into the darker corners of the human heart.

By 1913, the super-rich Rockefeller family was getting even richer with its Colorado Fuel & Iron Corporation, which employed more than twelve thousand coal miners in Colorado. Those miners were paid $1.68 a day and died at a rate twice as high as the national average. They lived in company towns, renting rooms at $2 a month or in hovels they built themselves. They often had to buy their own blasting powder or cut their own timbers. Sometimes the company paid them in "scrip," redeemable only at company stores where the prices were inflated. So the miners tried to form a union, which the Rockefeller family aggressively opposed.

On September 23, 1913, a union activist was murdered. That day, thousands of miners and their families walked off the job and moved out of the coal camp to makeshift "tent cities" at canyon mouths where they could control the influx of imported "scab" workers and to protest working conditions. The largest of those temporary camps was near Ludlow, Colorado, where miners sometimes dug protective "basements" beneath their tents in case violence broke out.

And it seemed likely. Rockefeller's men built the "Death Special," an armored car mounted with a machine gun that it used to clear out a tent camp in October 1913. Miners and strike-breakers were dying in isolated skirmishes. And Rockefeller had convinced Colorado Governor Elias Ammons to let his strike-breakers wear Colorado National Guard uniforms.

On April 20, 1914, National Guardsmen and strike-breakers led by General John B. Chase—a Denver ophthalmologist—fired machine guns into the Ludlow camp, and the miners fired back. The gun battle raged for fourteen hours.

In the midst of the fighting, a passing freight train stopped to let many of the miners and families board for a run to safety. Louis Tikas, a Greek union organizer at Ludlow, was arrested and killed by Guardsmen under the command of Lieutenant Karl Linderfelt.

Late in the day, the militia set fire to the camp and shot at anyone who moved. By the next morning, Ludlow was a charred mess.

Among the twenty-five dead were two women and ten children who had hidden in a "death pit" under a tent and suffocated in the fire. Thirteen other people—including three militiamen—died in the massacre. Sporadic violence continued at other camps for days.

It was all for nothing. The miners didn't win their demands and were all replaced by non-union workers. No strike-breakers or Guardsmen were ever prosecuted, although one strike leader was convicted of murder, and 408 miners were arrested.

But the Ludlow massacre electrified America and led to more union rights for workers and more laws to improve working conditions.

Today the site is marked with a memorial and interpretive displays. The "death pit" is preserved. The battleground has been scoured by government archaeologists, but the various artifacts—including children's toys, shoes, bullets, bottles, and cooking utensils—are seldom displayed anywhere.

Governor **Elias Ammons** (1860–1925) and General **John Chase** (1856–1918) are buried at Denver's Fairmount Cemetery, 430 South Quebec St. Ammons's grave is in Block 10, Lot 97, at GPS 39.70732, -104.89745; Chase is in Lot 9, Block 63, at GPS 39.70897, -104.90104.

Industrialist **John D. Rockefeller Jr.** (1874–1960) is buried in his family cemetery in Westchester County, New York. Despite the Ludlow tragedy, he was later celebrated as a social reformer and philanthropist.

Slain miner **Louis Tikas** (1894–1914) is buried in Trinidad's Masonic Cemetery at 13050 Nevada Ave. His grave is in the Knights of Pythias section at GPS 37.18708, -104.51190. His killer, **Karl Linderfelt** (1876–1957), is buried in the Los Angeles National Cemetery in California.

Two other interesting Ludlow figures are buried in unmarked graves in Trinidad's Masonic Cemetery. **William Snyder**, an eleven-year-old boy killed at Ludlow, is in Section 43, Lot 559, Row E5, or at GPS 37.18799, -104.51241. **Mack Powell**, a miner-turned-ranch hand killed in a crossfire the year before the Ludlow massacre, is buried in Section 19, Block 530, Lot 2, or GPS 37.18965, -104.51275.

Many of the funerals, attended by thousands of mourners, were held at the Holy Trinity Catholic Church, 235 North Convent St. in Trinidad, or GPS 37.168946, -104.506786.

The incident is covered in several books, including Scott Martelle's 2007 *Blood Passion: The Ludlow Massacre and Class War in the American West.*

MARSHAL BAT MASTERSON
Trinidad

Only twenty-nine, Bartholomew "Bat" Masterson (1853–1921) had been a buffalo skinner, Indian fighter, gambler, and lawman before he was hired in 1882 to clean up the rowdy town of Trinidad.

While he served in this job, his friends Wyatt Earp and Doc Holliday were involved in the infamous gunfight at the OK Corral in Tombstone, Arizona. Shortly afterward, Earp and Holliday came to

Trinidad, seeking Bat's help. Arizona wanted to try Holliday for murder, so Masterson arranged for Doc to legally stay in Colorado, facing fake charges that were never intended to go to trial. Doc Holliday never left and died a free man at Glenwood Springs five years later.

Masterson had his office on the top floor of the former Grand Columbian Hotel on the northwest corner of Main and Commercial Streets (GPS 37.168553, -104.505821). Built in 1879, it has been restored but is no longer a hotel.

Masterson left Trinidad after only a year. He worked a few more law enforcement jobs, was accused in a ballot-stuffing scandal in Denver, then managed the Denver Exchange in Creede before becoming a boxing promoter and sports columnist in New York City. In 1921, he died while writing a column in New York City. He's buried in Fairlawn Cemetery in the Bronx.

See also Doc Holliday's Grave ... Sorta (Glenwood Springs).

For one year, Marshal Bat Masterson kept his office in the top floor of Trinidad's Columbian Hotel.

VIRGINIA DALE STATION
Virginia Dale

The original station still exists about three miles off CR 43F at GPS 40.97372, -105.36613. This is private property, but you can see it from the public road.

The ill-tempered **Jack Slade** (1831–1864) never joined the pantheon of A-list outlaws like Jesse James or Butch Cassidy, but he exceeded them in cruelty. He killed his first man when he was thirteen.

By 1859, Slade had married the tough-as-nails Virginia Dale, an expert horsewoman and even better markswoman. In time, he became superintendent of the Overland Stage Company's line across some of the most lawless territory in the Wild West. Among the stage drivers he hired was fifteen-year-old William F. Cody, later to be known as Buffalo Bill.

His most important job was to make sure that the stages ran on time and were safe from desperadoes and Indians who harassed them. The brutal, ruthless Slade was the perfect man for the job.

As part of his job, Slade was determined to "discourage" an upstart trader named **Jules Beni,** who'd established a competing post he called Julesburg in northeastern Colorado (Julesburg I, the trading post site, is west of the modern city of Julesburg on private pasture land at GPS 40.941379, -102.362537). Slade suspected that Beni was not only poaching Overland customers and profits but also rustling Overland's animals.

When Slade visited Beni's post in 1860, the trader shot and wounded Slade, who vowed revenge. The next year, Slade bushwhacked Beni at his trading post, tied him to a fence post, shot him several times during a night of torture, then cut off his ears, which Slade made into a souvenir watch fob. (After several months, friends say Slade's grisly memento stunk so badly that most people couldn't bear to stand near him.) Nobody knows where Beni was buried.

In 1862, Slade established his headquarters at a stop he named for his wife, Virginia Dale. The one-story, hand-hewn log building has a stone fireplace, a stone-lined cellar, and a hand-dug well that's sixty-five feet deep. It is on the National Register of Historic Places.

In time, he tired of his job and reportedly began rustling and robbing stages. In 1864, Slade was lynched by vigilantes in Virginia City, Montana. Virginia claimed his body, which she kept pickled in alcohol—some say whiskey—under her bed until she could bury him in Salt Lake City. Virginia Dale eventually disappeared from history, although the stage station bearing her name remains one of the last Overland Stage structures still standing.

TEXAS SEVEN CAPTURED
Woodland Park

The Coachlight Motel and RV Park is at 19253 East US 24, or GPS 38.980556, -105.041111.

On December 13, 2000, seven dangerous inmates escaped from a maximum-security prison in Kenedy, Texas, fleeing with stolen clothes, a pickup truck, sixteen guns, and plenty of ammunition. Their leader was George Rivas, a brutal kidnapper and armed robber doing ninety-nine years; the others included two murderers, two rapists, an armed robber, and a child abuser.

Less than two weeks later, after a nationwide manhunt was launched, the Texas Seven killed rookie cop Aubrey Hawkins at an Irving, Texas, sporting-goods store, stealing $70,000, twenty-five weapons, and clothing.

On New Year's Day 2001, the gang rented a space at the Coachlight Motel and RV Park near Woodland Park. Within days, the *America's Most Wanted* TV show aired a segment about the escape, and on January 22, 2001, four of the escapees were captured at a Western convenience store just south of the RV park at GPS 38.962778, -105.029722; a fifth shot himself to death inside an RV. Two days later, the remaining two fugitives were captured in Colorado Springs.

George Rivas and Donald Newberry were convicted of killing Office Hawkins and are now on Texas's death row.

3

COLORADO WESTERN SLOPE

TED BUNDY IN COLORADO
Aspen

On January 12, 1975, Caryn Campbell—a twenty-three-year-old Michigan nurse vacationing in Aspen—forgot a magazine in her second-floor room at the Wildwood Inn in Snowmass Village (now Wildwood Lodge at 100 Elbert Lane, or GPS 39.206423, -106.954705). So she left her fiancé in the ski lodge's lobby, got on the elevator—and disappeared. More than a month later, her frozen and bludgeoned corpse was found in a snowbank a few miles from the lodge.

On March 15, 1975, ski instructor Julie Cunningham vanished while walking to a Vail tavern.

On April 6, 1975, Denise Oliverson of Grand Junction was riding her yellow bike to see her parents when she disappeared.

On April 15, 1975, high school student Melanie Cooley disappeared in Nederland, Colorado. Her half-nude body was found eight days later dumped by a roadside with a pillowcase tied around her neck and her skull crushed.

On July 1, 1975, Shelley Robertson, twenty-four, was seen talking to a strange man in a pickup at a Golden gas station. Her nude, decaying corpse was found two months later in an old mine shaft near Berthoud Pass.

Different women, different places ... but they might all share one grisly thing: Ted Bundy.

Bundy had been killing women since 1974, maybe earlier. He'd left a bloody trail from the Pacific Northwest to Utah, but investigators hadn't yet figured out they had a single murderer—much less

Colorado Western Slope

one of the nation's most prolific serial killers. And he had already killed at least fifteen women.

In January 1975, as the heat turned up in Utah where Bundy had killed four women in less than two months, he sought a new killing ground: Colorado. But by August he was back in Utah, where a routine traffic stop led to Bundy's arrest. Police found a ski mask, handcuffs, a crowbar, rope, an ice pick, and other burglary tools in his car. In his apartment, they also found a Colorado map with a check mark on the Wildwood Inn—where Caryn Campbell had been abducted seven months earlier.

In 1977, Bundy was convicted of an attempted kidnapping in Utah and extradited to face murder charges in Colorado.

While preparing his defense for the murder of Campbell, Bundy was allowed to visit the Pitkin County Courthouse's law library (506 East Main St., or GPS 39.190521, -106.817944), where he escaped through a second-story window. (As you face the front of the courthouse, the window is the second from the left on the second floor.) He was captured six days later but was already working on a new escape plan.

While awaiting trial at the Garfield County Jail in Glenwood Springs (now a parking lot at 7th Street and Colorado Avenue, or GPS 39.54768, -107.32652), Bundy sawed through a metal plate in his cell's ceiling and shimmied into the crawl space above, then to freedom. The jailer didn't even notice he was gone for seventeen hours.

Bundy made his way to Denver, where he hopped a flight to Chicago and, within days, to Florida. He was arrested in a stolen car on February 15, 1978, but not before he had killed four more Florida women. Ted Bundy never returned to Colorado. He was convicted and sentenced to die for his Florida murders. Oddly, his death row cell was next to serial killer Ottis Toole, who is linked to at least two murders in Colorado too.

Before he was executed in Florida's electric chair on January 24, 1989, Bundy confessed to killing Caryn Campbell. Her body was returned to her native Michigan.

After asking to use the Pitkin County Courthouse's law library, Ted Bundy escaped from its second-floor window, second from the left.

Bundy also revealed he had used crutches to approach Julie Cunningham, and asked if she'd help him carry his ski boots to his car. There, he clubbed her with his crowbar and handcuffed her. Her body was never found.

Bundy confessed to killing Denise Oliverson too.

When an investigator asked Bundy about Shelley Robertson, the killer replied, "I don't want to talk about that"; the case remains officially unsolved, but insiders strongly suspect Bundy.

Bundy never claimed responsibility for Melanie Cooley's murder and was implicated only by his known presence in the area. Investigators aren't convinced Bundy did it, but he remains a suspect.

If all five women were indeed killed by Bundy, they might not be his only Colorado victims. He confessed to killing more than thirty women, but nobody knows the exact body count, which might reach one hundred.

SPIDER SABICH MURDER
Aspen

Sabich's former home is at 372 North Starwood, or GPS 39.238093, -106.84983. It's in the exclusive neighborhood of Starwood, where access is closely guarded by gates and security patrols. It is the most private of private property.

Blond and blue-eyed ski champion Vladimir "Spider" Sabich (1945–1976) met Claudine Longet at a 1972 charity ski race in California. She was a pretty singer-actress recently divorced from crooner Andy Williams, and they fell in love. By 1974, Longet and her three kids had moved into Sabich's sumptuous stone-and-log chalet in the elite Starwood area. Inside, they had used beams from an old aerial ski tramway.

But over the next two years, Sabich's high living and Longet's insecurities took their toll. "It's either going to end," Sabich told a friend in 1976, "or we'll be married within a year." Locals were gossiping that the popular skier was considering evicting her and her kids from his house.

On March 12, 1976, Sabich was preparing to go to a party—alone—when Longet came into the bathroom and shot him once in the belly. He died in the ambulance with Longet beside him. Sabich, thirty-one, was buried at Westwood Hills Memorial Park in Placerville, California.

Longet, thirty-four, claimed the gun went off accidentally while Sabich was showing her how to use it. She was charged with reckless manslaughter, but a jury convicted her on a lesser charge of criminally negligent homicide. The judge gave Longet only thirty days in the Pitkin County Jail, which she served three months later—after a Mexican vacation.

After the murder, Longet was not the favorite celebrity in celebrity-rich Aspen. Locals, who'd never warmed to her even before Sabich's killing, wore T-shirts emblazoned with a picture of Longet with the words "Spider's Black Widow."

The Sabich family sued Longet but settled out of court. The settlement included a prohibition against Longet ever telling or writing her story.

HUNTING ACCIDENT OR MURDER?
Cedaredge

The hunting-camp murder scene is at GPS 38.622222, -108.615556.

You've heard of ballistics, DNA, and fingerprinting, but what about forensic *geology*? OK, maybe it's not the sexiest sleuthing science, but in addition to playing a role in the 1960 kidnap-murder of Adolph Coors III, it helped solve this case too.

On October 15, 1995, hunter John Bruce Dodson (1946–1995) was found shot to death while on a hunting trip with his newlywed wife, Janice, in Colorado's Uncompahgre Mountains. He'd been shot twice with a .308-caliber rifle.

Immediate suspicion fell on Janice's ex-husband, who was camped less than a mile away. The ex-husband claimed he was out hunting at the time of the shooting but that someone had stolen a .308-caliber rifle from his camp while he was gone.

Investigators searched in vain for the missing murder weapon for four years and the case went cold—until a volunteer searcher noticed bentonite clay that had lined a pond near the ex-husband's camp and remembered witnesses saying Janice was caked in mud at the time of the shooting.

Forensic geology proved that Janice had stepped or fallen in the unique mud near her ex-husband's camp—mud not found anywhere else within miles of the murder scene. That, plus Janice's collection of her husband's $500,000 life insurance policy, convinced a jury she killed him. She was sentenced to life in prison without the possibility of parole, and the Dodson case became one of the most fascinating cases in the history of forensic geology.

The murder was explored in Frank J. Daniels' 2006 book *Dead Center*.

See also Adolph Coors III Kidnapping and Murder (Morrison).

OUTLAW BOB MELDRUM ARTIFACTS
Craig

The Museum of Northwest Colorado is at 590 Yampa Ave., or GPS 40.515833, -107.5475. Hours are Mon–Fri 9–5 and Sat 10–4. Free admission; www.museumnwco.org.

"Bad Bob" Meldrum (1866–??) was a good outlaw and a bad lawman. In a career that included stints as a marshal, Pinkerton agent, union strikebreaker, and range detective, he was said to be more ruthless than Tom Horn and to have killed more people.

As the Old West evolved into a New West, Meldrum's skills as a brutal gunfighter were less in demand. He did time in the Wyoming Frontier Prison for killing a man in Baggs but emerged to become a saddlemaker in Walcott. He also became a skilled pen-and-ink artist.

The museum displays a Colt revolver engraved with Meldrum's name, a gift to him from a grateful Telluride mining company in 1904. The exhibit includes some of his illustrations and a holster hand-tooled by Meldrum.

Meldrum himself vanished after a fire destroyed his saddle shop near Saratoga, Wyoming, in 1926. His whereabouts and end remain among the minor mysteries for Old West buffs.

The museum also displays a gun that belonged to Wild Bunch outlaw Harry Tracy (1875–1902), who died in Oregon during a prison escape.

See also the Wild Bunch chapter.

1893 FARMERS BANK ROBBERY
Delta

The former bank site is at 316 Main St. (GPS 38.74260, -108.07090), although the bank building itself became a home at 319 Howard St. (GPS 38.74261, -108.06659).

Not much ever happened in Delta before September 7, 1893. That's when some Butch Cassidy and Cole Younger cohorts—Tom McCarty, brother Bill, and nephew Fred—robbed the Farmers and Merchants Bank. But they didn't get what they expected.

Tom waited in the alley behind the bank while Bill and Fred went inside to take the cash. But young Fred panicked and killed a teller. Bill and Fred fled, but Tom had already abandoned his kin when he heard the shots.

A local shopkeeper, Ray Simpson, grabbed his Sharps buffalo rifle and ran to see the commotion. He blew off the top of Bill McCarty's skull as he galloped away at full speed, then killed Fred with a second shot. Tom was already long gone.

According to the macabre customs of the day, Bill and Fred's corpses were propped up and photographed, then plopped in the same cheap box to be planted in the local potter's field.

Today the Delta County Historical Museum (251 Meeker, or GPS 38.74314, -108.06966) displays all the guns used that day, plus a few other artifacts. (Unrelated but interesting is a bridle braided by outlaw Tom Horn while he awaited his execution in Cheyenne, Wyoming.)

Dead teller **Andrew Blachley** (1847–1893) was buried in the Delta Cemetery, 1055 East 3rd St. His grave is in Block 1, Lot 11, or GPS 38.74485, -108.05484. The heroic marksman, **Ray Simpson** (1862–1940), is buried at Forest Lawn in Glendale, California.

In 1958, Blachley's eight orphaned sons placed a plaque at the bank site to commemorate the event.

Bill and Fred McCarty's grave is lost, but in 2001, when the townfolk realized the story had a little tourism value, a historical

Dead bank robbers Bill and Fred McCarty were dumped in a hole in the Delta cemetery and lost, although this interpretive marker is said to be close to their grave.

plaque and marker were erected in Delta Cemetery in their memory. It is at Block 2, Lot 180, or GPS 38.74590, -108.05544. The actual grave is believed to be within ten feet of the sign.

Historians believe Tom McCarty was killed in a Montana gunfight in 1900.

KOBE BRYANT HOTEL
Edwards

The Lodge at Cordillera is at 2205 Cordillera Way, or GPS 39.64313, -106.63441.

The sports world—not to mention Mrs. Bryant—was rocked when Los Angeles Lakers' superstar Kobe Bryant was accused of raping a nineteen-year-old hotel employee in Room 35 here on June 30, 2003.

For more than a year, the lurid case was the hot topic among sports fans and crime-watchers. Bryant tearfully admitted he'd had sex with the woman, who claimed it wasn't consensual at all. Bryant was facing up to life in prison and fines up to $750,000 if convicted.

But after a series of errors led to the accuser being identified publicly and her sexual habits being detailed in the media, she decided not to testify against Bryant. In 2004, the criminal charges were dropped, and a settlement was reached in a civil suit the woman filed against the basketball star.

Bryant resumed his basketball career without much damage. After the case was dropped, he signed a seven-year, $136 million contract and renewed his endorsement deals on his way to becoming the NBA's Most Valuable Player in 2008. He is still married too.

DOC HOLLIDAY'S GRAVE ... SORTA
Glenwood Springs

Linwood Cemetery (also known as Pioneer Cemetery) is at the intersection of Bennett Avenue and East 13th Street, on the east side of town. The trail to Doc's grave starts at the corner of Bennett and 12th Streets. It's about a half-mile climb on steep terrain, so wear comfortable hiking boots.

The mere mention of Doc Holliday conjures Old West images of Wyatt Earp, the OK Corral, and a dozen Hollywood movies. Doc was everything a mythic figure should be: smart, flawed, ruthless, dashing, loyal ... and short-lived.

John Henry Holliday (1851–1887) was trained as a dentist, but he came west around 1873 when he discovered he had tuberculosis. He opened a small dental practice in Dallas but quickly learned that gambling was more profitable. In 1877, Doc met a new friend, Wyatt Earp, in Fort Griffin, Texas, and they became inseparable—in life as well as in legend.

In 1881, Doc stood with his friend Wyatt and the Earp brothers in the infamous Gunfight at the OK Corral in Tombstone, Arizona—a

Doc Holliday's actual grave is lost, but this memorial goes to great lengths to celebrate Glenwood Springs' most famous—if brief— citizen.

deadly shootout sparked by an argument between Holliday and cowboy gang leader Ike Clanton.

He also rode with Wyatt on the "vendetta ride," in which they hunted down the men who killed Wyatt's brother Morgan. Doc was arrested in Denver for his role in one revenge killing, but with the help of his friends Wyatt Earp and Bat Masterson—then a marshal in Trinidad, Colorado—he was released after a couple weeks in jail.

Increasingly ill, Doc settled in Leadville in 1882, where he dealt faro in the Monarch Saloon (320 Harrison, or GPS 39.246938, -106.291153) and then at Hyman's Saloon (316 Harrison, or GPS 39.24680, -106.29113). Holliday was living in a room upstairs at Hyman's (in the northwest corner of the building) when he shot and wounded gunfighter Billy Allen in the bar. Holliday was acquitted and left town.

He moved around Denver for a while, growing frail. In 1887, a graying and feeble Doc Holliday took a second-floor room at Glenwood Springs' Hotel Glenwood (which burned down in 1945 at 732 Grand Ave., or GPS 39.546829, -107.324624). He hoped the town's curative hot springs would help him, but they didn't. Neither did his regular visits to the Mirror Bar (now a shoe shop at 714 Grand Ave., or GPS 39.547346, -107.324597), Doc's favorite saloon.

Bedridden on November 8, 1887, thirty-six-year-old Doc asked for a sip of whiskey and spoke his last words: "Now, this is funny." Some have speculated that he found it funny he was dying in bed without his boots.

Doc Holliday

It was midwinter in the Rockies, and the ground was frozen, so Doc's body was buried in a temporary grave in the area of 9th and Palmer Streets. It was reportedly moved later to an unmarked potter's field grave in Linwood Cemetery—although some people think he might never have been moved and lies now in somebody's backyard. Either way, some Georgia relatives came to retrieve his body in 1910, but nobody knew exactly where Doc lay. To this day, his grave's location is unknown.

But a memorial exists in the cemetery at GPS 39.53962, -107.32057. A marker on the spot says, THIS MEMORIAL DEDICATED TO DOC HOLLIDAY WHO IS BURIED SOMEPLACE IN THIS CEMETERY.

Also buried in Linwood is **Harvey "Kid Curry" Logan** (1867–1904), a Butch Cassidy gang member killed by lawmen. A marker (although not likely his actual grave in the potter's field) is at GPS 39.53911, -107.31859. See more in the Wild Bunch chapter.

MANSON VICTIM'S GRAVE
Glenwood Springs
Rosebud Cemetery is at 2301 Wolfson Rd. The grave is in Block 78, Lot 7, or GPS 39.51728, -107.32093.

Kindhearted musician Gary Allen Hinman (1934–1969) was working in a Los Angeles music shop when he met some members of Charles Manson's "family" in 1968. He let some of them live at his house in Topanga Canyon. But when Manson and his followers got too wild and weird, Hinman kicked them out.

On July 31, 1969, Hinman was found dead in his house, his face sliced open and two stab wounds to the chest. Eight days later, pregnant actress Sharon Tate and four house guests were slaughtered by members of the Manson family; the next night, Rosemary and Leno LaBianca were also viciously butchered. Manson minions Bobby Beausoleil and Susan Atkins got life sentences for killing

Hinman after another family member, Mary Brunner, testified against them.

Hinman's body was returned to his native Colorado for burial.

DIAMOND JACK ALTERIE'S HOTEL GETAWAY
Glenwood Springs

The Hotel Colorado is at 526 Pine St., or GPS 39.550828, -107.324898.

Chicago gangster Al Capone (1899–1947) and his sometime rival **Diamond Jack Alterie** (1886–1935) both loved the historic Hotel Colorado so much that the owners reportedly built a special canopy to hide their comings and goings from public view. According to the hotel, Alterie would often arrive in Lincoln convertibles, wearing a ten-gallon hat and silk shirt, and stroll around the lush grounds in expensive duds and glittering diamond rings—surrounded by tough bodyguards.

Alterie, who was a huge fan of everything Western, "retired" from the Chicago underworld in 1925. He owned all or part of several Colorado dude ranches, including one in Douglas County's Jarre Canyon, south of Denver, and the **Sweetwater Ranch** beside Sweetwater Lake, twenty miles northeast of Glenwood Springs (GPS 39.799922, -107.16691).

Today at the Hotel Colorado, you can even order Diamond Jack's Skillet, a ranch breakfast the mobster liked to serve his guests at the Sweetwater Ranch.

But in 1932, he got in a gunfight at the **Hotel Denver** (another Alterie hangout at 402 7th St. in Glenwood Springs, or GPS 39.54773, -107.323229). He wounded three men, prompting a judge to give him a choice: Go to prison or leave Colorado forever. Alterie un-retired, sold his ranches, and went back to Chicago for good.

Alas, it all ended when Capone went to Alcatraz in 1932 and Alterie was murdered in Chicago in 1935. Diamond Jack was buried at Forest Lawn Memorial Park in Glendale, California.

*Dude-ranching gangster
Diamond Jack Alterie loved
big cowboy hats.*

BULLDOZER RAMPAGE
Granby

The shed where Marvin Heemeyer built his armored bulldozer is a quarter mile west of town, just south of West Meadow Road at GPS 40.090293, -105.952658.

Marvin Heemeyer (1952–2004) was mad as hell and not going to take it anymore. After four years of battling with the town council, Heemeyer lost and a cement plant was built next door (GPS 40.090843, -105.953715). And to make matters worse, Heemeyer had bought a Komatsu D335A bulldozer to plow a road from his muffler shop (GPS 40.08985, -105.9521) to West Meadow Road, but the council quashed that idea too.

So for two years, Heemeyer closeted himself in his workshop, building a thirteen-foot-tall war machine. He encased his bulldozer in concrete-and-steel plates, wired it with closed-circuit cameras so he could drive without opening his airtight cabin, built powerful fans to keep his assault-rifle portals clear—and installed a cooler for his beer.

On June 4, 2004, Heemeyer started up his seventy-five-ton "killdozer" and drove it through the wall of his workshop. For the next hour, he lumbered through town, crashing through the concrete plant, the City Hall (Zero Jasper Ave., or GPS 40.08677, -105.94157), the bank (129 East Agate, or GPS 40.08584, -105.94057), the local newspaper office (424 East Agate Ave., or GPS 40.08487, -105.93536), and the local power company's office. In all, he destroyed thirteen buildings—and more than a dozen vehicles— and knocked out gas service while cops tried unsuccessfully to stop him with guns and grenades that didn't even slow him down.

Marvin Heemeyer secretly worked for months armoring his "killdozer" for a 2004 assault on Granby, Colorado.
Associated Press

Just when cops were asking for a National Guard Apache attack helicopter and a Hellfire missile, Heemeyer's dozer fell into the basement of a local hardware store at GPS 40.08511, -105.93513. Ten minutes later, he ended his rampage abruptly by shooting himself in the head.

It took twelve hours to cut through the armor plating to remove Heemeyer's body with a crane. The "killdozer" was cut up and sold for scrap in 2005.

Heemeyer was cremated and his ashes scattered by friends on a popular snowmobiling hill near Granby.

FAMILY KILLER'S HOME
Grand Junction

The Blagg home is at 2253 Pine Terrace Court, or GPS 39.08237, -108.63499.

On November 13, 2001, Michael Blagg called police to report his wife, Jennifer, and six-year-old daughter, Abby, missing. Even as the investigators searched the Blagg house for clues, he bragged that he was a born-again Christian and his life an open book.

Well, maybe a dirty book. Cops discovered Blagg had been visiting a local escort service for months and kept a considerable stash of porn in his house. They also found large amounts of blood in the master bedroom and the family minivan before one of Blagg's co-workers reported seeing him dumping two large cardboard boxes in the company dumpster. Then it was revealed that Jennifer, thirty-four, had recently claimed her husband abused her.

On June 4, 2002—almost seven months after she disappeared—Jennifer's corpse was found in the Mesa County Landfill (off Old Whitewater Road at GPS 39.011893, -108.491728). She had been shot in the left eye with a 9mm weapon. She was buried in her native Ardmore, Oklahoma … without Abby. The search continued unsuccessfully for little Abby for several more weeks before being

In 2001, self-proclaimed Christian Michael Blagg killed his wife and daughter in this suburban home, then dumped their bodies in the local landfill.

called off, but the Abby-Jennifer Recovery Foundation was formed to organize large-scale search efforts for missing children after the search for Abby ended.

In 2004, Michael Blagg, forty-one, was convicted of murdering his wife and abusing her corpse. He was sentenced to life in prison without the possibility of parole.

MOTHER-DAUGHTER SERIAL KILLER VICTIMS
Grand Junction

On July 25, 1975, twenty-four-year-old stay-at-home mom Linda Benson and her five-year-old daughter, Kelley, were found viciously stabbed to death in their Grand Junction apartment. Among the evidence were strange blood droplets on a cereal box and ashtray, but in the years before DNA testing, the case quickly went cold.

Linda and Kelley were buried in the same grave under the name Ketchum at the Municipal Cemetery, 263 26 1/4 Rd. Their grave is in Block 9, Lot 16, or GPS 39.04725, -108.56712.

Then in 2009, cold-case detectives submitted the blood evidence for DNA testing—and got a hit. The DNA profile allegedly matched Jerry Nemnich, a sixty-four-year-old Longmont trucker and ex-con with a long history of violent, sex-related offenses. He was suddenly also a suspect in the 1973 rape and murder of a University of Denver student. He was awaiting trial at press time.

LAWMAN "DOC" SHORES' GRAVE
Gunnison

Gunnison Cemetery is about a mile east of town on the north side of US 50. The grave is in Section 46, at GPS 38.54617, -106.89634.

Cyrus Wells Shores (1844–1934) was a lawman to the core. He'd worked as a railroad detective, a deputy U.S. Marshal, Salt Lake City's chief of police, and even rode with Tom Horn for a time. Called "Doc" because he was named for the doctor who delivered him, he was the sheriff of Gunnison County when he captured the accused cannibal Alfred Packer in 1874. His headstone reads: WESTERN COLORADO'S MOST NOTED FRONTIERSMAN, PIONEER AND LAWMAN.

See also Cannibal Camp (Lake City).

CANNIBAL CAMP
Lake City

The camp and graves are preserved about two and a half miles south of town beside CO 149 at GPS 38.00015, -107.29495.

Let's clear this up right away: He was born *Alfred* G. Packer on January 21, 1842, in Allegheny County, Pennsylvania. The Civil War broke out when Alfred was nineteen and he enlisted in the Union Army. He got a tattoo on his arm that misspelled his name as

Packer's grave in Littleton was eventually sealed in concrete to thwart Halloween pranksters.

Cannibal-killer Alfred Packer.

Alferd—an error he adopted as sort of a joke. However, whenever he signed his name, he typically signed *Alfred*—or just *Al*.

The second biggest mystery in Packer's life is not so easy to solve: Did he really kill and eat five companions at a remote camp in the Rockies in the brutal winter of 1874?

That February, against the advice of local Indians, Packer guided five would-be gold miners into the San Juan Mountains with only ten days' worth of food. When the group was stranded by a blizzard, the food ran out. According to Packer's later account, two men died of starvation and the rest ate their flesh to survive. Then a third died in an unspecified accident. Packer said he was off hunting firewood when one of the last two miners killed the other. When the last surviving miner tried to kill Packer, the guide claimed he killed his attacker in self-defense—and then ate parts of him until April, when he stumbled out of the mountains near Gunnison.

Packer was arrested in Saguache for their murders but escaped from the Saguache jail just before a search party found the remains of the five missing miners. They were buried on the spot.

*Alfred Packer was convicted of killing and
eating parts of five traveling companions
at this remote mountain camp in 1874.*

Packer lived on the lam in Wyoming for the next nine years. He
was arrested on a vagrancy charge in Fort Fetterman (near Douglas, Wyoming) and returned to Lake City to stand trial. Although he
claimed the killings and cannibalism were purely about survival,
he was convicted and sentenced to die. But the Colorado Supreme

Court overturned the sentence, and in a new trial, Packer got forty years for voluntary manslaughter.

Packer's was the first case of criminal cannibalism in U.S. legal history, but he'd be followed by the likes of Albert Fish (1870–1936), Ed Gein (1906–1984), and Jeffrey Dahmer (1960–1994).

In 1901, with the help of *Denver Post* muckraking columnist Polly Pry, Packer was paroled and moved to the small town of Deer Creek, west of Denver—and reportedly became a vegetarian. He died of senility in 1907 at age sixty-five and was buried in the Littleton Cemetery, 2552 West Ridge Court in Littleton. His grave is at GPS 39.60514, -105.01649 (look for his U.S. military marker under the tree nearest the secondmost northern entrance). The grave is covered with a concrete slab because local kids often celebrated Halloween by digging up Packer's corpse.

Archaeology at the camp on Cannibal Plateau has shown evidence that some of the men were eaten by humans, but nobody has found enough evidence to prove or disprove Packer's claims of self-defense.

Today the Hinsdale County Museum exhibits items related to Packer. It is at 130 Silver St. in Lake City (GPS 38.02769, -107.31783). It's only open in summer, Mon–Sat 10–5; Sun 10–4. Admission charged; www.lakecitymuseum.com.

Somebody at the Saguache County Museum at the southwest corner of San Juan Avenue and US 285 in Saguache, Colorado (GPS 38.08651, -106.142387) might tell you Packer spent time in the preserved 1908 jail there, but Packer was captured in 1874. He was actually held for questioning in a dungeon outside of town, from which he escaped.

The Museum of Western Colorado in Grand Junction (462 Ute Ave., or GPS 39.065663, -108.564931) exhibits a remarkable display devoted to Packer and the ongoing forensic examination of his crimes. It contains his guns, a hatchet and a bit of human skull excavated from the murder scene.

The truly tasteless tourist can grab an *El Canibal* burrito at the Alferd Packer Memorial Grill at the University of Colorado's Memorial Center, the corner of Broadway and Euclid in Boulder (GPS 40.006944, -105.271667).

And in Littleton, please look closely at his headstone. It says Alfred.

See also Polly Pry's grave in Fairmount Cemetery (Denver), Littleton Cemetery (Littleton).

MEEKER BANK ROBBERY
Meeker

The Bank of Meeker was at 594 Main St., or GPS 40.03734, -107.91347.

Not all bank robberies have happy endings for the outlaws ... especially in well-armed frontier towns.

On October 13, 1896, three former members of Butch Cassidy's Wild Bunch who'd formed their own gang strolled into the Bank of Meeker. When the clerk was slow in handing over the cash, robber George Law fired two warning shots while his two cohorts—Jim Shirley and "Kid" Pierce—stood watch.

But the two warning shots had alerted the townspeople, who quickly surrounded the bank with their own guns. The robbers emerged from the bank with some human shields, but the frightened hostages ran, and the robbers were quickly mowed down.

The three outlaws were buried side by side in the Highland Cemetery, a half mile south of town off CR 4. The graves are at GPS 40.03071, -107.91087.

Oddly, the White River Museum (565 Park Ave., Meeker, or GPS 40.038609, -107.913476) displays a Meeker Hotel guest register that robber Shirley signed before the crime.

*Three former Wild Bunch outlaws were killed by sharpshooting
locals when they tried to rob the Bank of Meeker in 1896.*

DID BILLY THE KID SLEEP HERE?
Meeker

The Meeker Hotel is at 560 Main St., or GPS 40.03741, -107.91309.

Lots of outlaws—Jesse James, John Wilkes Booth, Butch Cassidy among them—apparently enjoyed long lives after their supposed deaths, thanks to tireless mythmakers. And William H.
Bonney, aka Billy the Kid, one of the Old West's most infamous outlaws, was no different.

History tells us that Billy the Kid was killed by Sheriff Pat Garrett in New Mexico in 1881. In 1950, a Texan named Ollie "Brushy Bill" Roberts claimed to be the Kid and sought a gubernatorial pardon just before he died.

Did the real William H. Bonney sign the Meeker Hotel's guest register in the summer of 1889? It's said to be sealed inside a locked case at the White River Museum, 565 Park Ave., Meeker, or GPS 40.038609, -107.913476. Summer/fall hours 9–5 daily; winter hours 10–4 daily. Free admission.

STAR WITNESS AGGIE HENRY'S GRAVE
Meeker

Highland Cemetery is a half mile south of town, just east of CR 4. Henry's grave is in Section L-70 at GPS 40.03119, -107.91082.

In 1912, a coal mine owner named Gil Wesson, seventy, was murdered. The killer then torched Wesson's cabin to destroy the evidence.

The prime suspect was a man named Henry Goodell, whose dyspeptic disposition seemed to be the most damning evidence against him. A grand jury decided he had robbed and killed Wesson, so he was arrested.

That's when Aggie Watkins Henry (1880–1969) noticed the accused killer was wearing Gil Wesson's shirt. How could she be sure? She had mended the shirt just before Wesson's death with a small patch of material from one of her old dresses—which she still owned. Thus, Aggie became the star witness in one of northwest Colorado's most famous murder trials, held at the old courthouse (now Odd Fellows Hall) on the southwest corner of 5th and Main Streets (GPS 40.037412, -107.912478).

Goodell was convicted but escaped while being transported to the prison in Cañon City. Nobody knows what became of him.

Victim Gil Wesson (1842-1912) was buried in Highland Cemetery in section W-130, at GPS 40.03065, -107.91247.

Also in Highland Cemetery:

- **Buddy Roosevelt** (1898–1973) was not an outlaw but sometimes played one in the movies. A veteran of silent films who successfully transitioned to talkies, Kenneth Standhope Sanderson (his real name) appeared in more than 170 films in his career. His last movie was one of the best outlaw pictures of all time: *The Man Who Shot Liberty Valance*. His grave is in the Riverview I section, C4, at GPS 40.03178, -107.91103.

SABLE LAKE'S SECRETS
White River National Forest

Put on your hiking boots. To get there, drive thirty-nine miles on CR 8 from Meeker into the White River National Forest. Hike Trail 1821 from the Mirror Lake Trailhead (three miles) past Shamrock Lake, then three miles on Trail 1820 to Sable Lake. GPS: 40.0408, -107.3659.

In 1930, Hermie Parks's car broke down on CR 8 in the deep, dark mountain forest east of Meeker … and he vanished. A year later, Lester Burns's car broke down in the same area … and he vanished too. Searchers suspected the men had been killed and dumped in the nearby Sable Lake, a two-acre tarn that was only about twenty feet deep but at an elevation of nearly ten thousand feet. But when dragging and diving failed, the local sheriff decided to pump the entire lake dry. After dragging an enormous pump eight miles through roadless wilderness and building several support structures by hand from surrounding trees, searchers drained Sable Lake—and found nothing.

What happened to Hermie Parks and Lester Burns? Did they bump into a serial-killing mountain man? A hungry bear? Nobody knows, but the mystery won't die. The local sheriff has considered reopening the investigation more than eighty years later.

SOAP KETTLE MURDERS
Olathe

The farm where the bizarre killings happened is on the northwest corner of 5550 and Falcon Roads at GPS 38.592118, -108.05014.

In December 1917, farmer John Bush and his fourteen-year-old son, Otis, vanished from their place four miles west of town.

When police investigated, they found blood spatters everywhere and a pile of ashes containing human bones. A bizarre story emerged.

John Bush's mother, Nancy Jane Bush, claimed she'd caught grandson Otis stealing from her purse. She said that when she told her son, John beat Otis to death—then boiled the boy's corpse in a giant kettle used to make lye soap from animal fats.

Nancy Jane claimed she was so horrified that she later killed her own son, chopped him up and added him to the soap kettle's boiling contents, picking out bones and throwing them in the fire.

Police later found a bloody ax and thirteen empty lye cans on the farm, and then charged Mrs. Bush with murder. She was convicted and spent seven years in prison before being paroled. Locals say she spent the rest of her life in Delta, Colorado.

The grisly soap kettle, sold after the murders at a farm auction, still exists on an Olathe-area farm.

The soap kettle Nancy Bush used to boil down her son and grandson is still in the possession of an Olathe-area farmer.
Marilyn Cox

ENRON CEO KEN LAY'S DEATH
Old Snowmass, near Aspen

The rented house is at the Lazy O Ranch on Snowmass Creek Road, or GPS 39.306437, -106.979611. This is private property.

Disgraced as the swindling chairman of Enron and convicted of conspiracy and fraud in 2006, Kenneth Lay (1942–2006) was living in a rented ranch house on the thirty-two-acre Lazy O Ranch, owned by Pabst brewing heir I. V. Pabst, when he died of a heart attack on July 5, 2006.

Lay, who stole more than $43 million by lying about Enron's financial health before its 2001 bankruptcy, had sold most of his holdings to pay legal bills, including a 4,537-square-foot "vacation home" in Aspen (270 N. Spring St., or GPS 39.191823, -106.815036).

He and his wife had rented the four-bedroom, 2,038-square-foot farmhouse while he awaited sentencing for his crimes.

But Lay had a unique way of eluding justice: He died. By law, since he was not yet sentenced, his convictions were vacated as if he'd never committed the crimes.

Lay's body was cremated, and his ashes were reportedly buried in a secret location in the Colorado mountains. Lay's codefendant, CEO Jeff Skilling, is alive and in prison.

BUTCH CASSIDY'S FIRST "JOB"
Telluride

The former bank site is at 131 West Colorado Ave., or GPS 37.93735, -107.81150.

In 1889, Telluride's San Miguel Valley Bank was outlaw Butch Cassidy's first bank robbery. The bank burned in 1892 and was replaced by the Mahr Building. A plaque there marks the criminal occasion. For more details, see the Wild Bunch chapter.

4

BUTCH CASSIDY, THE SUNDANCE KID, AND THE WILD BUNCH

Imagine a dusty, faraway crossroads where Wild West history and myth intersect. Show up around sundown and you'll find Butch Cassidy and the Sundance Kid.

These two outlaws are so entangled in reality and legend that it's damn near impossible to unravel them without losing something important to their appeal. They exist in our American outlaw mythosphere as something more than men, yet something less than immortals, like affable ghosts who can never be freed from our attics.

Of course, they were common criminals, albeit slightly more successful than most. By the time they became the Wild Bunch in 1896, they were also better organized than the average outlaw gang. The gang seldom had more than ten riders, but membership was fluid, so the total number of men who rode with the Wild Bunch during its five years in existence could be in the hundreds. They stole thousands from banks and trains, vexed lawmen from New Mexico to Montana, and enjoyed a certain amount of admiration from poor folks along the way.

The myth-making started early. Almost nobody recognizes their real names: Robert Leroy Parker and Harry Longabaugh. Parker assumed a family friend's surname—Cassidy—and reportedly got the nickname "Butch" while working for a Rock Springs butcher who sold meat from stolen cattle. At twenty, Longabaugh was thrown in the Sundance, Wyoming, jail for stealing a horse in 1887 and was forever after known as the Sundance Kid.

Butch's best friend and sidekick in his early days was an outlaw named Elzy Lay, with whom he committed several crimes for seven years before they formed the Wild Bunch in 1896. They recruited loyal friends like Longabaugh, Will Carver, Ben Kilpatrick, Harvey Logan, and Sam Ketchum.

The first robbery credited to the Wild Bunch was the August 13, 1896, holdup of a bank in Montpelier, Idaho, a well-planned robbery that netted $7,165 and first revealed the gang's signature smoothness. More bank and train robberies followed, and the

Wild Bunch vs. Hole-in-the-Wall Gang

The terms are often used interchangeably to describe Butch Cassidy's loose-knit band of bad men, but are they really the same thing?

Technically, no.

The Hole-in-the-Wall Gang was a catch-all term for many outlaw bands that hid out in various parts of the vast Hole-in-the-Wall country west of Kaycee, Wyoming. It was not a single gang but many that used the relatively safe hideouts that dotted the area. Sometimes they worked together, but often they didn't. Among the notable outlaws who used the Hole-in-the-Wall were Jesse James and Black Jack Ketchum.

Butch Cassidy's crew called itself the Wild Bunch, and it was just one of several outlaw gangs taking refuge in Wyoming's Hole-in-the-Wall in the 1890s. In time, the Wild Bunch became the most notorious of all the gangs, and the two names became synonymous.

A moment of frivolity heralded the beginning of the Wild Bunch's end—and created one of the Old West's most unforgettable images. John Swartz

gang was suddenly getting the attention of Pinkertons and lawmen everywhere.

In June 1899, the gang robbed the Overland Flyer train near Wilcox, Wyoming, dynamiting the mail car and stealing $60,000 while a dazed clerk named E. C. Woodcock watched. A month later, the gang robbed a Rio Grande train near Folsom, New Mexico, of $70,000.

In August 1899, Lay was captured and sent to prison. Butch was morose and turned to the Sundance Kid for help, starting the close relationship that would become bigger than history itself.

Two weeks after Lay's arrest, the Wild Bunch held up the Union Pacific train at Tipton, Wyoming. Again, they blew open the safe and stole up to $55,000 while a young railroad clerk named E. C. Woodcock—yes, the same fellow—watched.

The heat was on the Wild Bunch, but as always, Butch had a plan. He dreamed of going to South America, where he imagined the pickings would be easier—and the lawmen fewer. To finance his plan, the Wild Bunch hit a bank in Winnemucca, Nevada, for $32,460. Several months later, the gang stole $65,000 from a train in Wagner, Montana—the last crime attributed to Butch Cassidy's Wild Bunch, which scattered after that.

In 1901, Butch and Sundance (with Sundance's girlfriend, a beautiful ex-teacher and hooker named Etta Place) sailed to Argentina, where they sustained themselves by ranching, mining, and robbery until they were reportedly ambushed at the small village of San Vicente by Bolivian *federales* after a 1908 payroll heist. Surrounded in a desperate gunfight, the two *gringos* were trapped. According to the troops, a grievously wounded Sundance was shot in the head by Butch, who then killed himself rather than be captured (not at all like the iconic ending to the movie). The corpses were buried together in an unmarked hole in the village graveyard.

That's where the legend would end except for an American fascination with resurrection.

In 1969, Paul Newman and Robert Redford starred in *Butch Cassidy and the Sundance Kid,* a romantic revision that bore little resemblance to facts but elevated the outlaws to the mythic stature of Robin Hood. The Sundance character played by Redford was actually a composite of Lay and Longabaugh. And the scene with

Etta Place riding on the handlebars of Butch's bicycle? It's based on a real event in which Butch gave madam Fannie Porter a ride on his bicycle in front of her San Antonio brothel.

Although Hollywood gave new life to Butch and Sundance, many people believed they actually returned from Bolivia and led long lives—just as Jesse James, Billy the Kid, and John Wilkes Booth supposedly eluded their historic deaths too. Decades before Elvis Presley was even born, Butch and Sundance were being sighted long after they'd reportedly died.

Wild Bunch experts Dan Buck and Anne Meadows have documented at least sixty different tales from three continents about how Butch and Sundance died. In some, they lived on as Wild West show performers, brigands with Pancho Villa, Washington entrepreneurs, or any number of romantic forms. If you believe the legends, they lived for many years, in many places, doing many things.

Science didn't help. Forensic anthropologist Dr. Clyde Snow of the University of Oklahoma led a 1991 expedition to Bolivia to exhume Butch and Sundance's bones, but they've never been found.

Many of Cassidy's relatives in the United States claim he visited them often after his alleged 1908 death, including at a 1925 family reunion.

And some say Butch came back to the United States as William T. Phillips (1863–1937) and started a business in Spokane, Washington. Phillips never claimed to be Butch, but he wrote a book about his friendship with the outlaw. His family said Phillips, on the brink of bankruptcy in the Depression, sortied to Wyoming and Utah looking for buried caches of outlaw money. He never found them and died of cancer on July 20, 1937. He's buried in Spokane.

Hiram Bebee (1867–1955) was a convicted cop-killer who did time in the Utah State Prison, but he claimed to be, in fact, the

Sundance Kid. Bebee died in prison in 1955 and is buried in the Salt Lake City Cemetery in Salt Lake City, Utah.

We might never disentangle fact from fiction in the case of the Wild Bunch. But myth is a real part of the Wild West, and without it, history might be less than the sum of its parts. Nonetheless, here are some real crossroads where Butch, Sundance, and the Wild Bunch passed on their way to immortality.

ROBERT BECOMES "BUTCH"
Rock Springs, Wyoming

In 1885, nineteen-year-old Robert Leroy Parker was calling himself "George Cassidy" when he took a job with Charlie Crouse, a Rock Springs rancher who also owned a butcher shop in town, where some say he was selling the meat of stolen cattle. Working in the shop at 432 Main St. (GPS 41.58642,-109.22023), Parker (aka Cassidy) got the nickname "Butch"—the moniker that would make him famous.

Although Butch Cassidy got little more than an alias from Rock Springs, a small exhibit about the outlaw at the Rock Springs Historical Museum (201 B St., or GPS 41.585299, -109.220613) includes some photos. The museum is open Mon–Sat 10–5. Free admission; www.rswy.net.

HARRY BECOMES "SUNDANCE"
Sundance, Wyoming

At age fourteen, Pennsylvania-born Harry Longabaugh went west, where he worked on several ranches from New Mexico to Wyoming. At age twenty, he grew tired of the cowboy's life and stole a horse in Crook County, Wyoming. Caught and convicted, he drew eighteen months at the Sundance jail—and a new nickname. And it appears he never worked another honest day in his life after his release.

The jail was torn down in 1972 to build a new courthouse at 309 Cleveland St. It stood on what is now known as Courthouse Green, a park immediately north of the courthouse at GPS 44.405563, -104.379044.

Today the Crook County Museum displays the court documents for Longabaugh's horse-theft trial and some furniture from the courthouse where he was tried. The museum is also at 309 E. Cleveland St. (GPS 44.40518, -104.378572). Summer hours are Mon–Sat 8–5; off-season hours Mon–Fri 8–5. Free admission.

In what might be a first, Sundance erected a statue to a criminal. A life-size bronze sculpture depicting the Sundance Kid in his jail cell stands at the corner of 3rd and Cleveland Streets (GPS 44.4048, -104.379049).

Some Sundance locals aren't too happy about a sculpture that celebrates the town's most famous inmate, Harry Longabaugh, aka the Sundance Kid.

WYOMING TERRITORIAL PRISON
Laramie, Wyoming

Robert Leroy Parker was a journeyman outlaw by the early 1890s. In a scheme more like the Mafia than the Old West, Parker promised—for a fee—to protect some Colorado ranchers from rustlers. But if they didn't pay, Parker and his buddies would rustle their cows. In 1894, stock detectives arrested Parker, who was convicted of rustling and served eighteen months of a two-year sentence.

Wyoming Governor William A. Richards (1849–1912) pardoned Parker in 1896 on the condition that this small-time rustler promise to never commit any more crimes in Wyoming. Oops. The gullible Richards's grave is in Cheyenne's Lakeview Cemetery, Pershing Boulevard and Seymour Avenue, at GPS 41.14417, -104.81114.

Wyoming Territorial Prison Park is at 975 Snowy Range Rd., or GPS 41.312222, -105.609444. Summer hours daily 9–6; call for winter hours. Admission charged; www.wyomingterritorialpark.com.

BUTCH CASSIDY'S FIRST "JOB"
Telluride, Colorado

In 1889, Telluride's San Miguel Valley Bank was the site of young outlaw Butch Cassidy's first bank robbery. Matt Warner, Tom McCarty, and Cassidy reportedly got away with $20,750 by thoroughly casing the joint first. The bank was at the northwest corner of Pine and Main/Colorado Avenue (GPS 37.93735, -107.81150). The original bank burned in 1892 and was replaced by the Mahr Building. A plaque there commemorates the occasion.

HOLE-IN-THE-WALL COUNTRY
West of Kaycee, Wyoming

As you might have already guessed, there are two specific geologic features that make this remote spot a perfect hideout for outlaws: a *wall* and a *hole*.

The "wall" is a red sandstone escarpment that protects a broad, grassy valley perfect for grazing cattle and horses—even stolen ones. The "hole" is a narrow gap in the red wall where outlaws could move their rustled herds in and out of the valley.

This isolated area—still primitive—was also ideal because no lawmen could sneak up without being seen.

It was used by many outlaw gangs from the late 1860s to around 1910. It was, in fact, an oddly successful outlaw commune, with several cabins, a livery stable, corrals, and supplies that were shared by many gangs, who were expected to contribute their fair share to its upkeep.

The Middle Fork of the Powder River carves through the valley, creating Outlaw Canyon. Deep inside is Outlaw Cave, reportedly used by the robbers to store their loot. It's at GPS 43.589619, -106.952505, accessible on a steep trail from the Outlaw Cave Campground on the rim above.

If you go, this ain't an easy Sunday drive. You should have a good four-wheel-drive vehicle, know a little about cross-country travel, and have plenty of water, food, and fuel.

To get to the "hole," take I-25 south from Kaycee to the TTT Road exit. At TTT Road, drive south about fourteen miles to Willow Creek Road (CR 111). Take this road west for about eighteen miles to CR 105, a primitive two-track road that bears north. As you travel along CR 105, you'll pass through several livestock gates that must be opened and, more importantly, closed. The "hole" is at GPS 43.546229, -106.830096.

The access road ends at the Hole in the Wall parking lot and trail head. A hiking trail to the "hole" is about two and a half miles on uneven terrain. Stay on the trail, which passes through private land, and close any gates through which you pass.

WILD BUNCH CABIN
Cody, Wyoming

A Hole-in-the-Wall cabin known to have been used by Butch Cassidy and the Sundance Kid has been preserved at Cody's Old Trail Town. The two-room log cabin was built on the Hole-in-the-Wall's Buffalo Creek in 1883 by Alexander Ghent, a sometime outlaw. The Wild Bunch often used this cabin—moved to Trail Town in 1973 and now displayed among twenty-six historic buildings built between 1879 and 1901—as a rendezvous site.

Old Trail Town (and the Museum of the Old West) is at 1831 DeMaris Dr., or GPS 44.515342, -109.103304. Summer hours daily 8–8. Admission charged; www.museumoftheoldwest.org.

History says Butch Cassidy often used this Hole-in-the-Wall cabin, although it has since been transported to Cody's Old Trail Town.

BROWNS PARK
Northwestern Colorado

Browns Park is a long, isolated valley at the remote corners of Colorado, Wyoming, and Utah. Some thirty-five miles long and five miles wide, and surrounded by canyons and rivers, it became a popular outlaw hideout in the late 1800s, so wild that the only law was said to be a fast gun.

Butch Cassidy was fond of the security in Browns Park—but he was equally fond of Ann Bassett, the wild and tough daughter of a local outlaw. (Some surmise that Ann was really the mysterious Etta Place since their physical descriptions are similar, but it is unlikely.)

Ann and Butch's relationship was off and on over the years. Butch even started courting Ann's sister Josie in the "off" times. Both women had significant presences in the Wild Bunch.

Butch occasionally worked at the Bassett Ranch.

Today the 13,455-acre Browns Park National Wildlife Refuge (headquartered at GPS 40.863889, -109.021944) lies on the northern edge of Dinosaur National Monument (headquartered at GPS 40.440278, -109.300833) in this far-flung, wild region.

ANN AND JOSIE BASSETT'S GRAVES
Browns Park, Colorado

Ann Bassett (1878–1956) loved her outlaws, but she finally settled down. After being acquitted in a rustling trial in which she earned the nickname "Queen Ann of the Rustlers," she married a prospector named Frank Willis in 1923. They settled down in a small Utah town, where she died on May 8, 1956. Her final wish was to have her ashes scattered over Browns Park, but her kindly husband couldn't bear to part with her, so he kept her ashes in his car trunk until he died in 1963. At that point, relatives buried her ashes in the Bassett family cemetery near the family ranch.

Ann and Josie Bassett, both romantically involved with members of the Wild Bunch at one time, are buried together in the family plot in Browns Park.

Josie Bassett (1874–1964) married five times and lived most of her life running her father's old ranch. Ironically, she lost most of her property to a land scam and lived the rest of her life in her modest cabin at GPS 40.425424, -109.17486. At age ninety, she broke her hip in a horse accident and died a few months later in 1964. She's also in the family cemetery.

The Bassett Family Cemetery is about a half mile north of CO 318, at GPS 40.77766, -108.84654. This cemetery is on private land and is only a hundred yards from the family's cabin, still in use today at GPS 40.77794, -108.84566.

POWDER WASH HIDEOUT
Powder Wash, Wyoming

Among the many hideouts used by the Wild Bunch and other outlaws was Powder Wash, another stop on the so-called Outlaw Trail. Its remote location between Robber's Roost in Utah and the Hole-in-the-Wall made it an excellent stopover for anybody trying to elude lawmen.

The old hideout is seventy miles southeast of Rock Springs, mostly on dirt roads. The site is five miles north of Powder Wash, Colorado, an oilfield man camp.

The Powder Springs "roost" was likely built in the 1880s by outlaw Dick Bender and his gang. It was later visited by notable badmen like Tom and Bill McCarty, Matt Warner, Harry Tracy, and other Wild Bunch gang members.

What will you see? If you have a four-wheeler or a horse, you can view the remains of a dugout likely built by Wild Bunch outlaw Matt Warner (GPS 41.00806, -108.29474); a cabin mostly still standing in a hollow that suggests it was used by people who didn't want to be found (GPS 41.026797, -108.27956); the remnants of other stone cabins from the outlaw period (GPS 41.03736, -108.27402); and a round corral dating to the same period (GPS 41.02729, -10827705). Archaeologist David Darlington believes one of the cabins was actually built by Butch Cassidy.

Here and there in this wide valley you can also spy a primitive fence made of limbs and tree trunks. Darlington believes it was created by the outlaws who lived there, to keep the herds they'd worked so hard to steal.

See also 1893 Farmers Bank Robbery (Delta).

MINER'S EXCHANGE SALOON
South Pass City, Wyoming

Butch Cassidy was a regular in the wide-open boomtown of South Pass City. Some say he liked to entertain the local women with his dancing at the dance hall, and some children grew up remembering the stout cowboy they called "Uncle Butch" standing

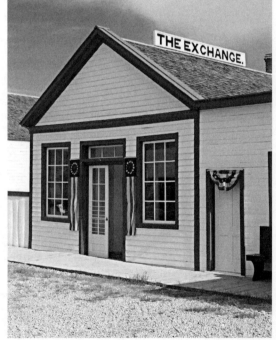

Old-timers once recalled "Uncle" Butch Cassidy pitching silver dollars to them from the door of the Miner's Exchange Saloon in South Pass City.

in the doorway of the Miner's Exchange Saloon (GPS 42.468202, -108.801223), flipping stolen silver dollars to them. The dance hall and the Exchange are both restored at the South Pass City Historic Site, two miles off WY 28, thirty-five miles south of Lander, Wyoming. It is only open May 15–September 30, daily 9–6; www .southpasscity.com.

THE HOLE-IN-THE-WALL BAR
Thermopolis, Wyoming

The centerpiece of this small-town museum is an elaborate cherrywood bar from an old Thermopolis watering hole known as Skinner's Bar. The saloon was a popular stop in the late 1800s for the Wild Bunch, mostly because the Hole-in-the-Wall country wasn't very far. The bar itself was handmade in Ireland but is known locally only as the "Hole-in-the-Wall bar." Whiskey is no longer served, but you can be sure that Butch, Sundance, and the rest of their gang bellied up there.

The Hot Springs Historical Museum is at 700 Broadway, or GPS 43.646376, -108.213894. Open summer hours, Tues–Sat 8–5; off-season 9–4. Admission charged.

WILCOX TRAIN ROBBERY
Near Rock River, Wyoming

On June 2, 1899, masked robbers barricaded the Union Pacific tracks about six miles west of the Old Rock Creek Station (no longer existing on private land at GPS 41.841757, -105.867058). After dynamiting a trestle, the robbers uncoupled some cars and pulled the express car two miles down the track. There, they ordered express-car attendant E. C. Woodcock to open the door, but he refused. So the bandits blew up the car, stunning Woodcock. They grabbed the safe and detonated it, too, snatching $30,000. Railroad bosses, the

Pinkertons, and newspaper reporters immediately suspected the Wild Bunch.

The robbery site, also on private land and barely accessible, is roughly at GPS 41.8561, - 105.8855.

TIPTON TRAIN ROBBERY
Near Tipton, Wyoming

Almost three months after the Wilcox robbery, a gang of masked raiders again stopped a train near Tipton, Wyoming. And again, mail clerk E. C. Woodcock was guarding the mail car. But this time, he opened the door before explosives were used. Harvey Logan reportedly blew the safe open but used too much dynamite. The robbers rode off with anywhere from $50 to $55,000, and again the Wild Bunch was suspected.

The robbery site is two and a half miles west of Tipton, at the tracks that run just south of I-80's exit 156 (GPS 41.628333, -108.31). Warning: This is an active, working railroad track on private property.

SHERIFF JOSIAH HAZEN'S GRAVE
Douglas, Wyoming

The Wild Bunch was often portrayed as nonviolent, but in reality members of the gang killed many people. One of them was Converse County Sheriff Josiah Hazen (1854–1899), who had tracked some of the Wild Bunch after the Wilcox train robbery. He was ambushed and killed near Kaycee, likely by Harvey "Kid Curry" Logan, one of the most violent gang members. The forty-five-year-old father of two was originally buried in Douglas's Pioneer Cemetery in a grand funeral, but his remains were moved in 1917 to the Douglas Park Cemetery, 9th and Ash Streets. His grave is at GPS 42.75706, -105.37631.

HARVEY "KID CURRY" LOGAN'S GRAVE
Glenwood Springs, Colorado

Iowa-born Harvey Logan (1867–1904) was known as the wildest of the Wild Bunch. He was a suspect in nine murders and at least seven robberies, and he escaped from jail twice. The Pinkerton Detective Agency once labeled him "the most feared and dangerous outlaw."

He called himself "Kid Curry" because of his close friendship with George "Flat Nose" Curry. In 1900, Flat Nose was killed by two lawmen while rustling steers in Utah—and Logan later killed one of them and a deputy in revenge.

Nobody knows exactly where Kid Curry was buried in Linwood Cemetery after his suicide, but a marker exists anyway.

A photo that purports to be a deceased Harvey "Kid Curry" Logan

The Wild Bunch broke up in 1901, but Logan continued his lawless ways. On June 7, 1904, he robbed a Denver & Rio Grande train near Parachute, Colorado. Two days later, he was wounded in a shootout with a posse. Rather than be taken alive, Logan killed himself.

He is buried at Linwood Cemetery (also known as Pioneer Cemetery) at the intersection of Bennett Avenue and East 13th Street, on the east side of Glenwood Springs. His unmarked grave is somewhere in the potter's field, but you'll see a marker in his memory at GPS 39.53911, -107.31859.

The pistol he used to kill himself is on display at Grand Junction's Museum of Western Colorado, 426 Ute Ave. (GPS 39.065705, -108.564941). As a bonus, this museum also displays cannibal Alfred Packer's hatchet and guns, a fragment of human skull from the massacre site, and several other historic outlaw artifacts.

BOB MEEKS'S GRAVE
Robertson, Wyoming

Wild Bunch member Henry Wilbur "Bob" Meeks helped Butch and Elzy Lay rob the bank in Montpelier, Idaho, in 1896. But the pathologically unlucky Meeks—who didn't wear a bandanna mask—was later captured and sent to the Idaho state prison.

On Christmas Eve 1897, Meeks escaped but left footprints in the snow and was recaptured. In 1903, he tried again but was shot in the knee, causing his leg to be amputated. Distraught and depressed, Meeks tried to kill himself twice (once with some scissors and once by jumping off a wall) but failed both times.

Meeks was sent to an insane asylum in Idaho, where he escaped a third time—but Idaho authorities let him go. His family later checked Meeks into the Wyoming State Hospital in Evanston, where he died on November 22, 1912. He was buried by family in Robertson, Wyoming. His unmarked grave is likely in the historic little cemetery on CR 279 (GPS 41.17508, -110.44592).

MCCARTY GRAVES
Delta, Colorado

In 1893, Cassidy buddies Tom and Bill McCarty (with Bill's son Fred) botched a robbery of the Farmers and Merchants Bank in Delta, Colorado. Tom escaped, but Bill and Fred McCarty were killed by angry citizens and buried without much respect in an unmarked grave at the Delta Cemetery. A historical plaque and marker have since been erected in Block 2, Lot 180, or GPS 38.74590, -108.05544, and the grave is presumed to be within ten feet of the sign.

MUSEUM OF THE MOUNTAIN WEST
Montrose, Colorado

Real Wild Bunch artifacts are few, but Butch Cassidy once sold his saddle and chaps at a Colbran, Colorado, ranch while trying to elude a posse. The items, made by Thompson Saddlery in Rifle, were later given to Cassidy's younger sister, who in turn donated them to the museum. The museum is at 68169 East Miami Rd., or the intersection of US 50 and East Miami Road, two miles east of Montrose, Colorado (GPS 38.487674, -107.813875). Open Mon–Fri 8:30–4:30. Admission charged; www.mountainwestmuseum.com.

SAN VICENTE CEMETERY
San Vicente, Bolivia

On the main road into town is a billboard: "Welcome to San Vicente: Here lie the remains of Butch Cassidy and the Sundance Kid." Here in this depressing little mining village, you can buy Butch and Sundance T-shirts, keychains, and other souvenirs. In 2008, on the macabre centennial of the famous outlaws' deaths, the town re-enacted their killing by Bolivian *federales*. The cemetery has roped off a section where the mortal remains of Robert Leroy Parker (1866–1908) and Harry Longabaugh (1867–1908) are presumed to lie, even though archaeological digs have failed to find them. Yet.

The cemetery is on the northern edge of town, at GPS -21.2642, -66.3155.

SUNDANCE KID'S GRAVE?
Casper, Wyoming

History abhors a vacuum. In the absence of any hard evidence about the fates of Butch and Sundance, resurrection myths abound. Butch's sister, Lula Parker Betenson, believed Harry Alonzo Longabaugh, aka the Sundance Kid, died in 1957 and was buried in Casper under the name of "Harry Long." Fact is, no graves in Casper's historic Highland Cemetery match the story. Oh, there's a "Harry Long" who died in 1923 (unmarked in Block 58, Lot 1, or GPS 42.84388, -06.30666) and a "Henry Long" who died in 1956 (Block 42, Lot 2, or GPS 42.84484, -106.30627), but like everything else with Butch and Sundance, we might just have to settle for the myth.

OTHER WILD BUNCH GRAVES

The Wild Bunch was a loosely knit crew. Members came and went, but a few names are more closely associated than others with the gang. Those buried outside Wyoming and Colorado are:

- **Etta Place** (b. 1878), unknown

- **Sam Ketchum** (1854–1899), Fairview Cemetery, Santa Fe, New Mexico

- **George "Flat Nose" Curry** (1871–1900), Greenwood Cemetery, Chadron, Nebraska

- **Tom McCarty** (1855–c. 1900), likely in Montana's Bitterroot Valley

- **Tom "Black Jack" Ketchum** (1863–1901), Clayton Cemetery in Clayton, New Mexico

- **Will "News" Carver** (1868–1901), Sonora Cemetery, Sonora, Texas

- **Harry Tracy** (1877–1902), Oregon State Penitentiary Cemetery, Salem, Oregon

- **Ben "The Tall Texan" Kilpatrick** (1874–1912), Cedar Grove Cemetery, Sanderson, Texas

- **Tom "Peep" O'Day** (died c. 1930), Pleasant Hill Cemetery, Dunlap, Iowa

- **Elzy Lay** (1868–1934), Forest Lawn Memorial Park, Glendale, California

- **Matt Warner** (1864–1938), Price City Cemetery, Price, Utah

- **Fannie Porter** (1873–c. 1940), unknown

- **Laura Bullion** (1876–1961), Memorial Park Cemetery, Memphis, Tennessee

FOR FURTHER READING

- *Digging Up Butch & Sundance* by Anne Meadows (1994, St. Martin's Press)

- *Butch Cassidy, My Brother* by Lula Parker Betenson (1975, BYU Press)

- *The Sundance Kid* by Donna Ernst (2010, University of Oklahoma Press)

- *The Outlaw Trail: A History of Butch Cassidy and His Wild Bunch* by Charles Kelly (1996, Bison Books)

- *In Search of Butch Cassidy* by Larry Pointer (1988, University of Oklahoma Press)

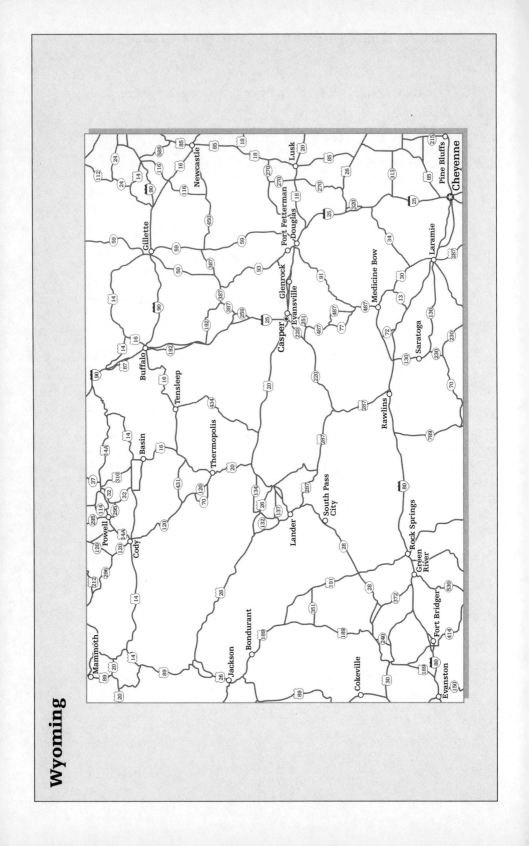

Wyoming

5

WYOMING

KILLER CORONER OR MURDER VICTIM?
Basin

Mount View Cemetery is on the north side of WY 30, about a mile west of Basin. The grave is in Lot 5, Block I, Supplemental Plot 4, or GPS 44.38779, -108.06271.

In the lurid tale of one-time coroner and casket salesman Don Cornett (1934–1982), many things aren't as they seem.

Hyattville native Cornett owned mortuaries in Basin and Casper, and he even served as the Natrona County Coroner from 1963 to 1967. He moved to California in 1970 and took a job as a traveling casket salesman. He sometimes bragged to coworkers how he could use his skills as a master mortician to manipulate a corpse's cause and time of death.

In 1981, the body of Donnie Sarafin, a seventeen-year-old male prostitute, was found in a shallow grave near Santa Cruz, fifty miles south of San Francisco. He had been bound, sodomized, and strangled, and the medical examiner estimated he'd been dead two to four days.

An eyewitness claimed that he'd seen Cornett pick up Sarafin in San Francisco, and cops found ropes and a handcuff key in his car's trunk, but Cornett had rock-solid alibis during the time of Sarafin's death. Nonetheless, police charged him with first-degree murder, believing Cornett had obscured the boy's true time of death by freezing his body, making it appear Sarafin had died much later than he did—and at a time when Cornett had alibis. When a hung jury couldn't decide Cornett's guilt, prosecutors planned to try him again.

But while awaiting his second trial, the newly admitted homosexual Cornett was busted for drugging a fourteen-year-old Sacramento boy and forcing him to have sex. In that case, a jury acquitted him. He'd dodged his second bullet.

The crafty ex-coroner's luck ran out a few months later when he started traveling with a male hustler in San Francisco. Soon after the pair holed up in a seedy Bay Area trailer that Cornett kept for his liaisons, neighbors found Cornett's corpse facedown on the floor, stabbed more than twenty times. His killer was never found.

Also see Spring Creek Raid (Tensleep).

LISA EHLERS MURDER SCENE
Bondurant area

The murder site is a turnout five miles north of Bondurant on the south side of US 191, or GPS 43.24549, -110.476681.

Just after dawn on June 21, 1984, twenty-seven-year-old Lisa Ehlers's body was found in a pool of blood beside her still-running car, in a highway turnout next to the Hoback River. She'd been shot in the head, chest, and hand. Her personal items and cash were still in the car. Ehlers had been on her way from Jackson to Florida to join her husband.

And that's where the case ended for investigators, who had no idea if she'd been killed by an opportunistic passerby, a passing serial killer, or somebody who knew her. The case went cold for twenty-five years.

Then an unexpected tip came from an even more unlikely source: the killer's son, who was in jail himself.

Troy Dean Willoughby was arrested, and the whole story began to fall into place. Witnesses said Ehlers had crashed a Jackson party and bought drugs from Willoughby, telling him she had to get money from her car. But as Willoughby watched, Ehlers drove off, presumably leaving Wyoming for good and skipping out on her drug debt.

An enraged Willoughby, then twenty-one, jumped in his car with two friends and raced after her. He caught up to her, and she pulled over to the side of the road. Willoughby dragged Ehlers from her car and shot her three times, killing her.

"That'll teach that bitch to rip me off," he told his companions.

Twenty-six years after the killing, Willoughby was convicted of first-degree murder and was sentenced to life in prison without the possibility of parole.

JOHNSON COUNTY WAR
Buffalo area

In the late 1800s, cattlemen were among Wyoming's richest and most influential citizens. They handpicked governors, judges, and legislators and grew wealthier as they expanded their ranches unchecked. They employed a small army of ruthless stock detectives—including Tom Horn and Frank Canton—to protect their interests.

Impromptu lynchings and intimidation of cattlemen's enemies hadn't stemmed the tide of homesteaders who owned small herds, so in 1892, the powerful ranchers embarked on a radical plan to build a small army and chase out real thieves and innocent small ranchers—demonized as "rustlers"—whom they believed threatened the prosperity of the cattle industry.

At the frigid daybreak of April 9, 1892, a small army of fifty men (plus a couple newspaper reporters) surrounded a small cabin on the KC Ranch, south of modern-day Kaycee. The "regulators" carried a hit list of cowboys and ranchers they intended to kill, and hired gunmen were offered a $50 bonus for every "rustler" they killed.

Two innocent trappers were captured, but two cowboys on the hit list—Nick Ray and Nate Champion—were murdered at the cabin. Before the Invaders—a name by which they became known—moved

Rustler or homesteader? Nate Champion
was the face of the "little guy" in the
Johnson County War, and paid with his life.

on to their next target, they pinned a note to Champion's bullet-riddled chest: "Cattle Thieves Beware."

The attack was witnessed by two local cowboys who rode back to Buffalo to sound the alarm. Sheriff Red Angus mounted his own angry posse to ride out and meet the Invaders.

Suddenly, the hunters became the hunted. The Invaders took refuge in the TA Ranch about thirteen miles south of Buffalo, surrounded by an infuriated mob bent on killing them all.

Faced with an unexpected debacle, Governor Amos Barber asked President Benjamin Harrison to intervene. Federal troops quickly quelled the two-day siege and "arrested" the Invaders, including leader Frank Wolcott, rancher William Irvine, Frank Canton, and a couple dozen hired guns from Texas—who were all eventually taken back to Cheyenne. Charges were brought against many of the regulators, but none was ever convicted.

Slain cowboys **Nick Ray** (1864–1892) and **Nate Champion** (1857–1892) are buried side by side in Buffalo's Willow Grove Cemetery, 351 North Adams Ave. Their graves are in Block 8, Section 7, or GPS 44.33401, -106.70262.

Their ambushed cabin no longer exists in a private pasture a quarter mile south of Kaycee on WY 196 (GPS 43.706667, -106.64). A historical marker beside the road explains the site's significance.

The 1891 bushwhacking of small rancher **John A. Tisdale** (1855–1891) helped trigger the Johnson County War. Tisdale was found in a gulch near his ranch (look for an iron cross at GPS 44.23899, -106.70437) and buried in Willow Grove Cemetery, Block 2, Section 4, or GPS 44.33374, -106.70189.

Powerful rancher **William Irvine** (d. 1924), a leader of the Invaders, is buried in Cheyenne's Lakeview Cemetery. His grave is in Lot 1090, or GPS 41.14420, -104.81174.

Governor Amos Barber (1861–1915), an invasion supporter who also testified that Tom Horn was the unlikely killer of Willie Nickell in 1901, is also buried at Cheyenne's Lakeview Cemetery. His grave is at GPS 41.14507, -104.81216.

Rancher John Tisdale was dry-gulched on this spot by an unknown killer in 1891, a prelude to the Johnson County War.

Sheriff **William "Red" Angus** (1849–1920) is buried in Buffalo's Willow Grove Cemetery. His grave is in Block 4, Section 18, or GPS 44.33375, -106.70414.

Invader **Frank Canton** (1849–1927), a stock detective who'd been a former Johnson County sheriff once suspected in the murder of John Tisdale, is buried in Fairlawn Cemetery in Oklahoma City. Invasion leader **Frank Wolcott** died in 1910 in Denver, Colorado.

The **TA Ranch**, where the invasion ended, is now a historic site and guest ranch on WY 196 about thirteen miles south of Buffalo (GPS 44.154587, -106.68731). Trenches used by Invaders and cowboys can still be seen, along with bullet scars on buildings. www.taranch.com.

In 1894, Wyoming newspaperman **Asa Mercer** (1839–1917) wrote the definitive account of the invasion, *Banditti of the Plains.* It revealed the political intrigues of the Wyoming Stock Growers Association, and as a result, Mercer got death threats, his reputation was destroyed, and he died in obscurity. The WSGA went so far as to destroy all but a few of the first-edition copies; even the Library of Congress's copy vanished. He is buried in the Hyattville Cemetery, one and a half miles northwest of Hyattville on the Alkali Road; the three-acre graveyard is a few hundred feet to the west. Mercer's grave is in Block 3, Lot 21, Row 11, or GPS 44.26508, -107.60621.

Texas A&M's Cushing Memorial Library in College Station, Texas, owns an extensive collection of legal papers related to the invasion, including bills of sale for cattle, letters. and trial documents.

A treasure trove of invasion artifacts—including Nick Ray's pistol and holster, an Invader's rifle, telegrams, letters, dioramas, and photographs—is displayed at the **Jim Gatchell Museum**, 100 Fort St. in Buffalo (GPS 44.34805, -106.69987). Summer hours daily Mon–Sat 9–6 and Sun 12–6; off-season hours Mon–Fri 9–4. Admission charged; www.jimgatchell.com.

A bronze statue of Nate Champion greets visitors at the entrance.

Kaycee's **Hoofprints of the Past Museum** also offers interpretive displays, books, and a statue of Nate Champion. It's at 344 Nolan Ave. (GPS 43.710794, -106.639255). Open June–Oct, Mon–Sat 9–5 and Sun 1–5. Free admission; www.hoofprintsofthepast.org.

The short-lived but deadly Johnson County War was not just a significant historical event but soon became an integral part of the Western mythos. The conflict between big ranchers and homesteaders has formed the basis of many Western novels and films, such as Owen Wister's 1902 novel *The Virginian,* Jack Schaefer's 1949 novel *Shane* and the 1953 movie of the same name, Walter van Tilburg Clark's 1940 book *The Ox-Bow Incident,* and director Michael Cimino's grotesquely expensive and horrendously inaccurate 1980 film *Heaven's Gate.*

See also Outlaw/Lawman Tom Horn (Cheyenne); Lynching of Cattle Kate (Casper); Killer Bill Booth Hanged (Buffalo); Historic Occidental Hotel (Buffalo); Owen Wister Country (Medicine Bow).

HISTORIC OCCIDENTAL HOTEL
Buffalo
10 North Main St., or GPS 44.347057, -106.699208.

Built in 1880 near the historic and well-traveled Bozeman Trail, the Occidental has a legendary reputation in both fact and fiction.

Over the past 130 years, its guest list has included Buffalo Bill, Teddy Roosevelt, and Ernest Hemingway. It has also hosted more than a few outlaw figures, from Calamity Jane and Tom Horn to Butch Cassidy and Sheriff Frank Canton. But two of its most famous guests—one real and one imaginary—are inextricably linked to the historic grand hotel.

Western author Owen Wister (1860–1938) was a frequent guest at the Occidental, where he liked to watch the Western characters who passed through. Many of them found their way into his novels, including his masterpiece, *The Virginian* (1902).

In fact, in that groundbreaking book, the Virginian's final gunfight with bad guy Trampas—the first "walk-down" in the history of Western literature—takes place on the street in front of the Occidental.

The hotel fell on hard times during the rise of the car culture after World War II and barely survived until the 1980s, when it closed. But in 1997, just before the historic old building was to be torn down, a local couple bought the building and has now returned the Occidental to its former frontier luster. You can even stay in the fully restored Owen Wister Suite, where it's believed he wrote some of *The Virginian*.

The historic Occidental was the setting for the first classic gunfight in American fiction—between the Virginian and Trampas.

See also Owen Wister Country (Medicine Bow); Killer Bill Booth Hanged (Buffalo); Outlaw/Lawman Tom Horn (Cheyenne); and the Wild Bunch chapter.

KILLER BILL BOOTH HANGED
Buffalo

The gallows stood just outside the back door of the Johnson County Courthouse, 76 North Main St. The approximate location of the one-time gallows is GPS 44.34764, -106.69985.

Bill Booth (d. 1886) left a trail of bodies wherever he went. He killed his wife and child in Oklahoma, an African-American cowboy in Colorado, a German trapper in Wyoming—and others.

But he underestimated the determination of Johnson County Sheriff Frank Canton, one of the Wild West's most dogged and feared lawmen.

When Booth was caught with a stolen horse in Miles City, Montana, Canton quickly had him returned to face murder charges in Buffalo. Canton got Booth to confess during the long stagecoach ride back. Booth proved to be a crafty escape artist, but Canton was always one step ahead of him.

Tried and convicted, Booth was sentenced to be hanged. On the day of his execution, he was walked out back to a temporary gallows and within a few minutes became the only outlaw ever legally executed in northern Wyoming. One onlooker remarked that Booth was "the best looking man at the hanging."

Booth's body was buried in an unmarked grave in the town cemetery's potter's field. Most of that cemetery's graves were later moved to Willow Grove Cemetery, but no record exists of Booth's exhumation. He likely remains buried someplace under the homes built where the old cemetery had been.

Frank Canton (1849–1927), who started his career on the wrong side of the law as a bank robber and cattle rustler, later became a range detective who played a big role in the so-called Johnson County War in 1892. He also was a marshal in the Yukon during the gold rush, marshal for "Hanging Judge" Isaac Parker in Arkansas, and a hero of dime novels. He died in 1927 and is buried in Fairlawn Cemetery in Oklahoma City.

ROLLER-RINK MADAM
Buffalo
The saloon and brothel were on the southwest corner of Main and Angus Streets (now a parking lot at GPS 44.345188, -106.698441).

In Johnson County's first recorded land transaction, widowed Iowa farm wife Nettie Wright bought a half interest in a one-story log saloon on Main Street and within a couple years, it became known as Nettie's Place. It provided after-hours "recreation" to soldiers from nearby Fort McKinney, including carnal pleasures.

To stay one step ahead of her competitors in the saloon business, Nettie added Wyoming's first roller-skating rink to her bar. In February 1885, she bought forty-five pairs of roller skates from Kansas City at $1 per pair.

When Nettie died, she was buried in Buffalo's old cemetery with an expensive headstone. Most of that cemetery's graves were later moved to Willow Grove Cemetery, but no record exists of her exhumation or whatever happened to her headstone. Like executed killer Bill Booth, Nettie likely remains buried under the homes built where the old cemetery had been.

FREMONT CANYON BRIDGE MURDER
Alcova Lake area, thirty-five miles southwest of Casper
The Fremont Canyon Bridge spans the North Platte River between the Pathfinder Dam and Alcova Reservoir about thirty-five miles

*Towering twelve stories above the North Platte, this bridge
was the site of the rape of one young Casper girl and
murder of another in 1973, a crime that still haunts the city.*

**southeast of Casper. It is on Fremont Canyon Road/CR 408
(which veers west off CR 407 south of Alcova) at GPS 42.471232,
-106.79625.**

On a chilly late-September night in 1973, sisters Becky Thomson,
eighteen, and Amy Burridge, eleven, were abducted from a grocery

store parking lot (now a neighborhood church at 1220 South Melrose St. in Casper, or GPS 42.838381, -106.309285) by two small-time crooks, Ron Kennedy and Jerry Jenkins. For hours, the knife-wielding thugs drove them around town, beating and terrorizing them.

Sometime around midnight, Kennedy and Jenkins drove the girls to Fremont Canyon Bridge, a remote span over a deep, dark gorge. Kennedy first threw young Amy off the twelve-story bridge into the river below, killing her instantly. Then Kennedy and Jenkins took turns raping Becky before throwing her, too, off the towering bridge.

But Becky didn't die. Half-naked, with a broken pelvis and other injuries, she managed to swim to the riverbank, where she hid until dawn. At first light, she miraculously dragged her wrecked body up the treacherous, rocky canyon wall and was found by fishermen.

She was able to identify Kennedy and Jenkins, who were convicted in 1974 of first-degree murder and rape, then sentenced to die. Their death sentences were commuted to life in prison when Wyoming's death laws were declared unconstitutional in 1977— and suddenly they were eligible for parole after three years on Wyoming's death row.

Becky Thomson, who had not recovered from the monstrous crime, sunk deeper into her fear that the two would someday get out of prison and return to kill her. Survivor guilt, drug abuse, and emotional issues took their toll. In 1992, Becky returned to the scene of the crime and leaped off Fremont Canyon Bridge. Her suicide sent a shock wave through her hometown.

Becky's ashes were buried in her sister Amy's grave at Casper's Highland Cemetery at 4th and Conwell Streets in Casper. The grave is in Block 182, at GPS 42.84180, -106.30247.

Jenkins died in prison of a heart attack in 1997. His ashes were buried secretly in his father Edgar's grave at Natrona Memorial Gardens, 7430 West Yellowstone Hwy. in Casper. His grave is at GPS 42.88346, -106.43846.

Ron Kennedy remains at the Wyoming State Penitentiary in Rawlins, where he occasionally comes up for parole.

The story was explored in Ron Franscell's 2008 book *The Darkest Night*.

See also Wyoming State Penitentiary Cemetery (Rawlins).

LIL MISS MURDER
Near Casper

Old Government Bridge is about twenty-two miles southwest of Casper on WY 220, or at GPS 42.638266, -106.617787. The old bridge is just east of the highway as it crosses the North Platte River.

On March 25, 1988, eighteen-year-old Lisa Marie Kimmell got into her new black Honda CRX with a personalized license plate that read LILMISS and started out on a trip from Denver to Billings, Montana, to visit her family.

But she never got there. Along the way, Kimmell was stopped for speeding near Douglas, then vanished.

Eight days later, fishermen found her seminude body floating in the North Platte River at Old Government Bridge. The coroner found that she'd been bound, beaten, and raped for at least six days before she was bludgeoned, stabbed six times, and dumped into the river. The case quickly went cold. Kimmell's black Honda CRX was still missing, and clues were scant.

Then a handwritten letter was left on her grave in Billings' Sunset Memorial Cemetery, saying (in part), "you're always alive in me." It was signed "Stringfellow Hawke," Jan-Michael Vincent's character in the TV show *Airwolf*.

In 2002, cold-case detectives took another look at the Lil Miss case after fourteen years. DNA collected from Kimmell's body matched a convicted kidnapper named Dale Wayne Eaton of Moneta, Wyoming, who was in a federal prison in Colorado. His handwriting matched the note left on the grave, and a neighbor told police she'd seen Eaton digging a large hole in his front yard just days after Kimmell disappeared in 1988—a water well, he told her. When investigators dug into the hole, they found Kimmell's long-lost Honda CRX, still bearing the LILMISS license plate.

In 2004, Eaton was convicted of first-degree murder and now awaits execution on Wyoming's death row. The Kimmell family won Eaton's Moneta property (GPS 43.16386, -107.72309) in a wrongful-death lawsuit and on July 18, 2005—what would have been Lisa's thirty-sixth birthday—they burned his house to the ground. Ash debris and scattered remnants of the trailer remain today, but it is on private land.

Eaton is suspected in several other similar murders between 1983 and 1997 in which young women were abducted and later found dead—including the disappearance of Lander's Amy Wroe Bechtel in 1997—but has never been charged.

The Kimmell case is detailed in Lisa's mother Sheila Kimmell's 2005 book, *The Murder of Lil Miss.*

LYNCHING OF CATTLE KATE
Casper area

The lynching site is believed to be in Pine Canyon, just off Spring Gulch, about one mile east of Independence Rock at approximately GPS 42.487396, -107.101293. You might see photos of old trees in that area, but the hanging tree fell decades ago. This is private property.

Wild West history has almost as many star-crossed love stories as range wars, but the tragic romance of Ella Watson and Jim Averill is both.

Canadian-born **Ella Watson** (1861–1889) was just a teenager when her family homesteaded in Kansas. She married but fled her abusive husband four years later, starting on a lonely odyssey that led to Rawlins, Wyoming, where she worked as a boardinghouse waitress.

There, she met **Jim Averill** (1851–1889), a former soldier and surveyor who owned a ranch and roadhouse on the Sweetwater River, just east of Independence Rock. Ella soon moved to Averill's ranch, filed her own land claim, and soon had her own ranch. Between them, Watson and Averill owned 320 acres—infuriating the bigger ranchers that surrounded them.

It was a bad time to make cattlemen mad. Many small ranchers were settling in Wyoming, cutting profits and rangelands for big ranchers. All-powerful and ruthless, big cattlemen were quick to accuse any nuisance neighbors of rustling or, in the case of Ella Watson, trading stolen cattle for sexual services. There's little evidence Ella Watson actually stole cattle or worked as a prostitute, but the rumors spawned her nickname: Cattle Kate.

Averill was a nuisance too. As an experienced land surveyor, he questioned the legality of some neighboring ranchers' claims. He even wrote a scathing letter to the local newspaper, accusing some cattlemen of illegally enlarging their holdings with bogus homestead claims.

By July 20, 1889, the ranchers had had enough. Six men rode out to "arrest" Watson and Averill as rustlers. They were loaded into a wagon and taken to a remote gulch. There they were dragged to a large rock beneath a pine tree and hanged.

Their corpses were left hanging in the July heat for two and a half days. A Casper reporter described the scene:

> *Hanging from the limb of a stunted pine growing on the summit of a cliff fronting the Sweetwater River were the bodies of James Averill and Ella Watson. Side by side they swing, their arms touching each other, their tongues protruding and their faces swollen and discolored almost beyond*

*recognition. Common cowboy lariats had been
used, and both had died by strangulation, neither
fallen over two feet. Judging from signs too plain
to be mistaken a desperate struggle had taken
place on the cliff, and both man and woman had
fought for their lives until the last.*

Their bodies were cut down and taken to Averill's roadhouse, where they were buried. Today that site is flooded by the waters of the Pathfinder Reservoir.

A coroner's jury found that six area ranchers had hanged Watson and Averill. They were arrested and all posted $500 bonds—but the charges were dismissed when witnesses suddenly became scarce.

The lynching is considered among the first big volleys of the great Wyoming range war that escalated to the 1892 Johnson County invasion and the 1909 Spring Creek Raid near Tensleep.

The day she died, Kate bought a pair of moccasins from a band of Shoshone Indians camped beside the Sweetwater River. Today they are displayed at the Wyoming State History Museum, 2301 Central Ave. in Cheyenne (GPS 41.139427, -104.818022).

Rancher **Tom Sun** (1844–1909), a former trapper and Army scout who was among the six lynchers, never denied his participation. His ranch, six miles west of Independence Rock and now owned by the Mormon Church, became a National Historic Landmark in 1960. He is buried in the Rawlins Cemetery, 915 Third St. His grave is at GPS 41.79749, -107.23958.

The murder is detailed in George Hufsmith's 1993 book *The Wyoming Lynching of Cattle Kate*. In 1980, Cattle Kate and Jim Averill's story got completely twisted and inextricably tangled up in the Johnson County War—which actually happened a few years later—in Michael Cimino's epic-failure Hollywood blockbuster, *Heaven's Gate*.

See also Johnson County War (Buffalo); Spring Creek Raid (Tensleep).

CHARLIE WOODARD LYNCHED
Casper

Highland Cemetery is at 4th and Conwell Streets, or GPS 42.846217, -106.304569.

On New Year's Day 1902, Natrona County Sheriff Charlie Ricker, a popular ex-Army scout who had been born in England, rode out to arrest Charlie Woodard, who'd escaped jail while awaiting a burglary trial.

But Woodard didn't go peacefully; he killed Ricker and escaped again.

Woodard was eventually captured and brought back to Casper amid a swirl of rumors that he'd be lynched as soon as he arrived. Up to five hundred angry citizens waited for Woodard when he arrived on the train, and a few small boys reportedly sprinted through the crowd shouting, "Hang him!" But nobody tried to lynch him.

Woodard got a fair trial and was sentenced to be hanged on March 28, 1902. But impatient locals couldn't wait. The day before his official hanging, vigilantes broke into the Casper jail, bound and gagged the jailer, then hanged Woodard a few hours before his formal appointment on the gallows. They left him dangling for all to see, a note pinned to his blouse: "Process of law is a little slow, so this is the road you have to go. Murderers and sinners beware! People's Verdict."

Sheriff **Wilson Charles Ricker** (1841–1902) was buried in a grand funeral in Highland's Block 34, Lot 16, or GPS 42.84491, -106.30625.

Charlie Woodard was buried nearby with less pomp (and an unmarked grave) in Block 3, Lot 8, or GPS 42.84388, -106.30666.

OUTLAW/LAWMAN TOM HORN
Cheyenne

History doesn't always have all the answers, but that doesn't mean people don't keep asking.

Even as a kid, Missouri-born **Tom Horn** (1860–1903) was a crack shot and an expert tracker. As a man, his skills—including his cold-blooded calculation—made him one of the Old West's most enduring legends. But no matter how hard Horn was, he couldn't survive the coming of a New West.

Horn ran away from home as a teenager and was a scout during the Arizona Apache wars. He drifted, riding in the rodeo and working a silver mine, until he was hired by the Pinkerton Detective Agency in 1891.

The rise of big cattle operations in Wyoming—and homesteaders streaming into Wyoming's wide-open lands—created a need for "enforcers" or "regulators" who roamed the range to intimidate and kill anyone who threatened the big ranchers. Tom Horn was well

After Horn's 1903 hanging, his brother buried him in Boulder, Colorado.

Awaiting execution, Tom Horn reportedly braided the rope used to hang him.

suited to the work and was hired as a stock detective in 1892. He quickly became one of the most feared and ruthless men who ever held the job.

Just past dawn on a the foggy morning of July 18, 1901, fourteen-year-old Willie Nickell rode his father's horse to a gate on the family ranch forty miles northwest of Cheyenne. Three shots rang out, two hitting the boy's back. Willie stumbled seventy-five feet toward home before he dropped dead on the road.

While a secret stenographer recorded every word in this office, Marshal Joe LeFors coaxed a drunken Tom Horn into damning admissions about the Willie Nickell murder.

The Nickell family had imported three thousand sheep into cattle country at a time when cattlemen expected free range. Historians speculate that Willie's killer had actually been gunning for the boy's father, Kels Nickell, a sheepman who had irked local cattlemen, including Horn's employer, John C. Coble.

The crime scene—one of Wyoming's most significant—is marked but little known. After the killing, Kels Nickell placed a circle of stones around the spot where his son died, and almost a century later, the University of Wyoming placed a modest concrete marker there too (GPS 41.682643, -105.22586). But even if this weren't jealously guarded private property, it's instructive to know that even people who know the exact spot routinely get lost in the rugged terrain and tangle of dirt roads. Best advice: Don't go.

Willie Nickell (1887–1901) was buried in Cheyenne's Lakeview Cemetery, the southeast corner of Pershing Boulevard and Seymour Avenue. His grave is in Lot 950, or GPS 41.14445, -104.81248. His father, **Kels Nickell** (1855–1929), is buried beside him.

Dogged lawman (or dishonest bumbler, depending on who's telling it) **Joe LeFors** (1865–1940) suspected Horn in the killing of the Nickell boy. After drinking with Horn—who had a reputation of loose talk when drunk—LeFors took Horn back to the Cheyenne U.S. Marshal's office to chat. A hidden stenographer wrote it all down—including Horn's comment, "It was the best shot that I ever made and the dirtiest trick that I ever done."

The U.S. Marshal's office where Horn "confessed" was at 216-218 West 16th St. (also known now as Lincolnway). As you stand on the street below, the office was behind the ornate second-floor bow window (GPS 41.132506, -104.816134).

Horn's legal defense was paid by his friend and employer **John Coble** (1859–1914). His lawyer was former Wyoming Supreme Court Justice **John W. Lacey** (1848–1936). Both are buried in Lakeview Cemetery. Coble committed suicide in 1914 and is at GPS 41.14540, -104.81236; Lacey is at GPS 41.14575, -104.81054.

One of the witnesses in his trial was **Dr. Amos Barber**, a former governor of Wyoming (and a pro-cattleman figure in the Johnson County War), who said Willie Nickell's fatal wounds could not have been inflicted by Horn's .30-.30-caliber rifle. Barber (1861–1915) is buried in Lakeview Cemetery, Lot 1165, at GPS 41.14507, -104.81216.

Horn claimed he wasn't in the area on the day Willie Nickell was killed, that his confession was just drunken bravado, and that key details didn't match Horn's confession. In fact, no physical evidence existed against Horn.

But even a high-powered defense, logic, and respected witnesses couldn't save Horn from his own damning words. After Horn was convicted by a jury, **Governor Fenimore Chatterton** faced huge pressure to commute the death sentence, but he refused—and lost the next election. Chatterton (1860–1958) is buried at GPS 41.14358, -104.81181 in Lakeview Cemetery.

Did he do it? Expert historians disagree about Horn's guilt in Willie Nickell's killing—but nobody disputes that Horn was a hired gun who'd killed many others.

On November 20, 1903, Horn was hanged in the county jail (which was torn down to build the new county courthouse, 309 West 20th St., or GPS 41.135675, -104.818883). He had escaped briefly from jail but was recaptured. Legend says he spent his last weeks braiding the rope that killed him, but the story is probably apocryphal; he braided mostly bridles and other tack, experts say. He spoke his last words to the county clerk who helped him into place: "Ain't losing your nerve, are you, Joe?"

The corpse of the forty-two-year-old outlaw—already a legend—was claimed by his brother, who buried him in Columbia Cemetery, 9th and Pleasant Streets in Boulder, Colorado. John Coble paid for an ornate coffin, and the family posted a guard in the cemetery for weeks to thwart grave robbers whom they feared might put America's most famous stock detective on the sideshow circuit. Horn's headstone—which bears his wrong birth year—is at GPS 40.0075, -105.2836.

Horn was among the first men hanged with a unique gallows designed by Cheyenne architect **James P. Julien** (d. 1932). The execution is triggered when the condemned man steps on a trap door; his weight opens a valve under the scaffold and water is emptied from one vessel to another. When the transfer is complete, counterbalances spring the trap door and the condemned man falls through. The gallows were later moved to the Wyoming Frontier Prison (500 West Walnut, Rawlins), where it was used in executions until 1937. It is still displayed in the prison-museum's death house (GPS 41.793267, -107.24338).

Julien is buried in an unmarked grave in Lakeview Cemetery at Lot 2101, Section F, or GPS 41.14581, -104.81026.

Horn's 1894 Winchester rifle (Serial #82667) was briefly displayed at a Cheyenne museum but is now back in the private hands of the family to whom he bequeathed it before his hanging. Is it the murder weapon? If Horn shot Willie Nickell at all—and some experts say he probably didn't—it would be very difficult to prove, because he owned several high-powered rifles and no bullets have ever been found for any ballistics analysis.

Famous lawman Joe LeFors—who also chased Butch Cassidy's Wild Bunch—is buried in Buffalo's Willow Grove Cemetery. His grave is in Block 51, Section 8, or GPS 44.33296, -106.70412.

Charles Ohnhaus (1880–1952), the clandestine stenographer who sealed Horn's fate, was also buried at Cheyenne's Lakeview Cemetery. His grave is in Lot 1017, or GPS 41.14400, -104.81155.

The Wyoming State Archives, 2301 Central Ave. in Cheyenne (GPS 41.139427, -104.818022), holds all the original trial evidence.

Colorado's Delta County Historical Museum (251 Meeker in Delta, or GPS 38.74314, -108.06966) displays one of the bridles braided by Horn while he awaited his execution.

Horn's life and death are detailed in Chip Carlson's 2001 book *Blood on the Moon*. Horn's story was also highly romanticized in the 1980 film *Tom Horn*, starring Steve McQueen.

RICHARD JAHNKE MURDER
Cheyenne

The murder house is at 8736 Cowpoke Rd., or GPS 41.19890, -104.80970.

Life in the Jahnke house was a living hell. Richard Jahnke, an IRS agent and survivalist, abused his wife and his children,

Tyrannical father Richard Jahnke was killed by his son in front of the garage at this house in 1982.

physically and sexually. And they suffered in silence … until they couldn't.

On November 16, 1982, Jahnke fought with his sixteen-year-old son Richie, ordering him to leave the family home. That night, Jahnke and his wife went out to dinner and returned after dark. As he was opening his garage door, he was killed by several shotgun blasts from inside, and the assailants fled through a bedroom window.

By morning, Cheyenne police had arrested two suspected killers: Jahnke's children, Richie, sixteen, and Deborah, seventeen.

"I shot my father for revenge," Richie told police that morning. He explained how he'd armed himself with one of his father's shotguns and waited inside the garage. Deborah waited in the living room with a .30-caliber automatic carbine, just in case her father eluded Richie's attack.

At trial, horrifying details emerged of Richard Jahnke's myriad abuses, discipline, and uncontrollable outbursts—occasionally abetted by his battered wife. Richie even testified that just before the shooting, Deborah came into the garage and asked if they should shoot their mother too. Richie refused.

A jury convicted the siblings of voluntary manslaughter. Richie was sentenced to five to fifteen years in prison but was freed by then-Governor Ed Herschler after only two years. Deborah was sentenced to three to eight years in prison as an accessory, but her sentence was commuted too. She changed her surname to Alexander.

The case was examined in Alan Prendergast's 1986 book *Poison Tree: A True Story of Family Violence and Revenge*.

ARMY SNIPER KILLS WIFE
Cheyenne

The Old Chicago Restaurant is at 1734 Meadowland, or GPS 41.159099, -104.799078.

Budding singer Robin Munis and her soldier husband, David, were in the midst of a bitter divorce in July 2007. When his harassing phone calls became too much, she called the cops, who warned David to calm down.

The next night, while forty-year-old Robin was singing with her band at the Old Chicago Restaurant, David snapped. He parked his black pickup about one hundred yards away and fired a single shot from his high-powered sniper's rifle through the restaurant's back door, hitting his estranged wife in the head and killing her instantly.

David, thirty-six, escaped to rugged Rogers Canyon, outside Laramie. Four days later, as forty cops, dog teams, and a Blackhawk helicopter closed in on his remote camp, David shot himself.

Robin Munis was buried in Tennessee; David Munis's remains were cremated in his native Montana.

FILMMAKER ALLEN ROSS'S MURDER
Cheyenne

The house where Ross' body was eventually found is at 303 East 17th St., or GPS 41.134833, -104.812202.

In 1995, when Chicago filmmaker Allen Ross was shooting a documentary about the Mississippi River, he abruptly disappeared. His friends and family searched for him, but clues were few.

They learned that Ross had met a woman named Linda Greene at a class in Chicago. He had moved with Greene to Oklahoma, where she led a religious cult called the Samaritan Foundation, which believed (among other things) that talking on a telephone allowed vampires to gain control over people.

But what they didn't know was deadly. Greene and her followers moved around a lot. When they ran into legal problems in Oklahoma, they relocated to a peaceful Cheyenne neighborhood where they kept a low profile.

Five years after he disappeared, filmmaker Allen Ross's body was found in a crawl space of this Cheyenne home.

Ross had apparently married Greene and followed her from place to place until 1995, when he threatened to leave her. Shortly after that, Ross disappeared, and the cult broke up.

In 2000, Cheyenne police found Ross's body crammed in the crawl space of the 17th Street house where the cult had lived communally. He'd been shot once in the head.

Cops suspected Linda Greene, but she died in 2002 in Arkansas of natural causes before they could charge her. Instead, they charged another cult member, who spent two years in prison for helping to bury Ross.

Ross's body was buried in Naperville Cemetery, Naperville, Illinois. In 2001, German filmmaker Christian Bauer—who sometimes worked with Ross—made *Missing Allen*, a documentary about Ross's disappearance and murder.

AMERICA'S FIRST WOMAN JUDGE
Cheyenne

Lakeview Cemetery is at the southeast corner of Pershing Boulevard and Seymour Avenue. The grave is at GPS 41.14399, -104.81185.

Esther Hobart Morris (1814–1902) wasn't exactly a militant feminist or even a legal thinker, but in 1870 she was appointed the Justice of the Peace in the boomtown of South Pass City, making her the first woman judge in American history.

Morris had been an Illinois farm wife and milliner before her husband moved to the gold camp at South Pass and opened a saloon. Among the twenty-seven cases she handled in her eight months on the bench (none overturned): an assault and battery charge against her husband, who was known as a mean drunk.

After she left office, Morris became a stellar figure in the women's suffrage movement. She died in Cheyenne at age eighty-nine. Her stone is simple and bears only her name and dates. Bronze statues at the U.S. Capitol's Statuary Hall and the Wyoming Capitol pay tribute to her.

Also in Lakeview Cemetery:

- **Governor Amos Barber** (1861–1915), who authorized the invasion of armed militia in the 1892 Johnson County War, a range war between homesteaders and big cattlemen. His grave is at GPS 41.14507, -104.81216 .

- **Governor William A. Richards** (1849–1912), who pardoned a small-time rustler named Butch Cassidy in 1869 on the condition that Butch promise to never commit any more crimes in Wyoming. A slight miscalculation. His grave is at GPS 41.14417, -104.81114.

- Tom Horn's young victim, **Willie Nickell** (1887–1901), who was murdered by a long-shot sniper at age fourteen, likely mistaken for his father, **Kels,** (now buried beside him). Horn was eventually hanged for the Nickell killing. Several other key figures in the life and times of Horn are buried here too. The Nickell graves are in Lot 950, or GPS 41.14445, -104.81248.

See also Johnson County War (Buffalo); Wild Bunch chapter; Outlaw/Lawman Tom Horn (Cheyenne).

BUFFALO BILL HISTORICAL CENTER
Cody

This collection of five museums is at 720 Sheridan Ave., or GPS 44.525064, -109.073006. Summer hours are daily 8–6; off-season hours vary slightly. Admission charged; www.bbhc.org.

This sprawling complex dedicated to the art and history of the Old West exhibits surprisingly little on the outlaw past, but you can find a few curiosities, such as *Gunsmoke* Marshal Matt Dillon's pistol and holster and Palladin's pistol and holster from *Have Gun Will Travel.* The extensive firearms collection—built around the Winchester Collection—contains many of the guns favored by both outlaws and lawmen. Art lovers can also see Frederic Remington's *Guard of the Bullion Stage* and Charles M. Russell's *Attack on the Wagon Train,* among others.

See also Earl Durand's Rampage (Powell).

SCHOOLHOUSE BOMBING
Cokeville

Cokeville Elementary School is at 250 North Sage St., or GPS 42.08700, -110.95396.

Once the only cop in the tiny ranching town of Cokeville (pop. 650), David Young was fired for being overzealous. He disappeared for a while but returned in May 1986 with an apocalyptic plan.

On May 16, 1986, Young and his wife, Doris, casually parked in front of Cokeville Elementary School and unloaded three gasoline bombs, nine handguns, and four rifles. Young, forty-three, marched into the school office and announced, "This is a revolution!" while Doris, forty-seven, gathered 167 kids into a first-grade classroom.

While holding the terrified children at gunpoint, Young demanded $2 million per hostage and an audience with President Reagan—or he would "wipe out Cokeville."

Cops and anxious townsfolk quickly surrounded the school. After a two-and-a-half-hour standoff, David left the classroom to go to the toilet. He handed Doris one of his crude bombs—two bottles of gasoline wired to a detonator. While he was gone, Doris accidentally set it off.

Later analysis showed the bomb had malfunctioned. If it had exploded at full force, it would have demolished the entire side of the school building and killed everyone in the room.

Instead, the stunted blast ignited some children's clothing and burned many of them, but none were killed. Stunned teachers shoved the kids through the classroom's blown-out windows to safety while a wounded Doris writhed in agony.

David rushed back to the classroom, wounding a teacher in the back. He put Doris out of her misery with a single gunshot through the brain, then turned the gun on himself. The couple's remains were buried in Idaho.

Several of the children later told investigators they'd seen angels in the classroom that day, including many who recalled a "beautiful lady" who told them to stand near the window.

The bombing is detailed in Cokeville parents Hartt and Judene Wixom's 1994 book *When Angels Intervene to Save the Children*, which was adapted into the 1994 CBS TV movie *To Save the Children*.

A disgruntled ex-cop and his wife took the children of Cokeville Elementary hostage in a massive bomb plot that went seriously wrong for the perpetrators.

CHARLIE STARKWEATHER CAPTURED
Douglas

The actual arrest site is near Orin Junction, fourteen miles southeast of Douglas, at approximately GPS 42.656777, -105 .200958.

The placid American heartland was stunned in January 1958 when a nineteen-year-old Nebraska kid named Charles Starkweather and his fifteen-year-old girlfriend, Caril Fugate, went on a weeklong killing spree across two states.

It all began on January 21 when Starkweather—who'd killed a young service station attendant less than two months before—killed Fugate's mother, stepfather, and two-year-old sister because the parents wouldn't let him see their daughter. Caril helped him hide the bodies, and they embarked on a deadly journey in Starkweather's stolen Packard across Nebraska in which they killed six more people.

On January 29, Starkweather and Fugate were in Wyoming, where Fugate reportedly killed traveling salesman Merle Collison as he slept in his car beside the road (the approximate site is on CR 29/Sunflower Trail west of Douglas at GPS 42.78575, -105.56612). They tried to escape in Collison's car, but it stalled at almost the same moment Natrona County Deputy Sheriff Bill Romer drove up. Fugate leaped from the car and ran toward Romer's cruiser, screaming, "He's going to kill me!"

Starkweather fled in his Packard, and Romer radioed ahead while he took Fugate to safety.

In Douglas, Police Chief Bob Ainslie and Sheriff Earl Heflin piled into a squad car and chased Starkweather at speeds up to 110 mph. Ainslie pulled up close to Starkweather's Packard near Orin Junction, and Heflin leaned out the passenger window to fire four shots from his Winchester .30-.30 pump-action rifle, grazing Starkweather's neck with one bullet. When Starkweather saw his own blood, he slammed on the brakes and surrendered.

"He thought he was bleeding to death," Heflin told reporters. "That's why he stopped. That's the kind of yellow son of a bitch he is."

While Starkweather was held in the old Converse County Jail (razed to build a new hospital at GPS 42.759237, -105.38102), Wyoming Governor Milward Simpson vowed that if convicted, the young killer would not be executed in Wyoming—which only quickened Starkweather's extradition to Nebraska.

In May 1958, he was convicted and died about a month later in the Nebraska electric chair. He was buried in Lincoln's Wyuka Cemetery—where five of his victims were also buried.

Fugate was also convicted of murder but received a life sentence with a possibility for parole. Although her role in the killings is murky, she almost certainly participated (Starkweather himself said she killed some of their victims). Fugate was paroled in 1976 and lives today in Michigan. She refuses to talk about the murders.

Deputy Romer (1928–1991) later became the Natrona County Sheriff. He is buried in Natrona Memorial Gardens, 7430 West Yellowstone Hwy. in Casper. His grave is at GPS 42.88369, -106.439012.

After their careers ended, Chief Ainslie died and was buried in Nebraska, and Sheriff Heflin died in 2003 and was cremated. Starkweather's last victim, Merle Collison (1923–1958), is buried at Mount Olivet Cemetery in Great Falls, Montana.

DOC MIDDLETON'S GRAVE
Douglas

Douglas Park Cemetery is at 9th and Ash Streets, or GPS 42.75610, -105.37500. The grave is at GPS 42.75604, -105.37473.

Rustler James Middleton Riley (1851–1913) got the nickname "Doc Middleton" because he was so good at "doctoring" brands on cattle and horses. He's been credited with stealing more than two thousand horses during a single two-year period in the 1880s.

He's also legendary for his role in the famous 1893 man-and-horse endurance race between Chadron, Nebraska, and Chicago, Illinois (for that year's World Fair)—a race in which he secretly rode a train.

In 1913, Doc Middleton was jailed for running an illegal saloon in Douglas. He died there, either from a gangrenous infection or a stabbing. Nobody knows for sure.

Also in the Douglas Cemetery:

- **George Pike** (d. 1908), an Iowa-born thief and rustler who stocked his Wyoming ranch with stolen animals. He was also famous for his barroom shooting demonstrations, in which he'd bet he could shoot a man's vest buttons off across the length of a saloon. He was a popular cowboy because ranchers reckoned as long as they employed Pike, he wouldn't steal their cows. GPS 42.75608, -105.37506.

- Sheriff **Josiah Hazen** (1854–1899), who was shot and killed near present-day Kaycee, Wyoming, while trying to arrest a gang of train robbers, including the Wild Bunch's Harvey Logan. He was originally buried in the old Pioneer Cemetery north of Douglas but moved here in 1917. GPS 42.75706, -105.37631.

See also the chapter about the Wild Bunch.

WYOMING POLICE ACADEMY
Douglas

The academy is at 1556 Riverbend Dr., just west of WY 59, or GPS 42.76839, -105.408631.

All of Wyoming's state, county, and local police are trained at the Wyoming Law Enforcement Academy.

The academy is also home to the Wyoming Peace Officers Memorial, which pays tribute to all lawmen who die in the line of duty. At this writing, sixty-three names appear on the memorial wall, starting with Deputy Robert Widdowfield and railroad detective H. H. Vincents, both killed in 1878 while chasing "Big Nose" George Parrott and his gang of train robbers near Rawlins. Parrott was later lynched by angry citizens.

See also Big Nose George Becomes a Pair of Shoes (Rawlins).

JACK HUMPHREY MURDER
Evansville

The house is at 211 Copper St., or GPS 42.86115, -106.27441.

It might have looked like an open-and-shut case, but for twenty-nine long years, the murder of thirty-year-old Jack Humphrey (1947–1977) was a cold case.

On November 23, 1977, Jack was found dead in his upstairs bedroom in the small Casper suburb of Evansville. He'd been shot in the back of the head with his wife's .243-caliber hunting rifle—which was later found (with an empty shell casing) in a snowbank ten feet outside the house's back door. Jack had been having problems with his wife, Rita, and they were in a financial bind. Other than his wife, who claimed to be asleep on a downstairs couch when she heard the fatal shot, only his small children were in the house.

But deputies came up empty. Some even suggested it was just an odd suicide, even though a coroner's inquest called it murder. Three years after the killing, Rita Humphrey was arrested, but charges were dismissed for lack of evidence. Ten years after her husband's killing, authorities gave the murder weapon back to Rita, and it was promptly lost—along with most of the sheriff's records of the case.

The case went cold until 2002 when new evidence came to light. Jack's body was exhumed, and murder charges were again filed against Rita Humphrey, who promptly argued that her right to a speedy trial was violated. The Wyoming Supreme Court disagreed, and she was convicted of second-degree murder in 2006. She's now serving a twenty-five- to forty-year sentence at the women's prison in Lusk.

Jack Humphrey was buried in Natrona Memorial Gardens, 7430 West Yellowstone Hwy. in Casper. His grave is in Garden of Love 50A-2, or GPS 42.88301, -106.43939.

EXECUTED KILLER MARK HOPKINSON'S GRAVE
Fort Bridger

Fort Bridger Cemetery is one mile south of Fort Bridger on Cemetery Road, at the northwest corner of its intersection with CR 219. The grave is in a family plot at Lot 868 on the western edge of the old cemetery, at GPS 41.30333, -110.38516.

On August 7, 1977, a bomb was thrown through the window of Evanston lawyer Vincent Vehar's home, killing him, his wife, and his son. A simple water dispute was about to unfold into one of Wyoming's most complex criminal cases.

The mastermind behind the bombing was Mark Hopkinson, an ex-con who headed a loosely knit band of trailer-park thugs. He had ordered one of them to kill Vehar, a lawyer for the local water board with which Hopkinson was quarreling.

The convoluted plot unraveled after one of Hopkinson's cohorts, Jeffrey Green, told investigators about the Vehar killing and testified against Hopkinson in an unrelated bombing incident. Hopkinson was sent to federal prison, where he immediately began plotting Green's death.

On May 20, 1979, shortly before Green was to testify against the imprisoned Hopkinson in the Vehar bombing, Green's tortured body was discovered at a highway rest area with more than one hundred cigarette burns and a gunshot wound in his neck. He was also buried in Fort Bridger Woodmen Cemetery's section 196F, at GPS 41.30223, -110.38477. To date, his actual killers have not been found.

Eventually, Hopkinson was convicted of killing the Vehars and Green and sentenced to die by lethal injection.

Proclaiming innocence to the end, Mark Hopkinson (1949–1992) died by lethal injection at the Wyoming State Penitentiary on January 22, 1992, Wyoming's only condemned inmate to be executed since Andrew Pixley in 1965.

The Vehars were buried together at the Evanston City Cemetery, 526 County Rd., about a mile north of town. The graves are in the Catholic cemetery's Block 6, Lot 6, Spaces 3-4, or GPS 41.28097, -110.96196.

See also Andrew Pixley Murders (Jackson).

FOOD FIGHT GONE BAD
Fort Fetterman

The Fort Fetterman State Historic Site is just east of WY 93, eleven miles north of Douglas. The unmarked grave is somewhere inside the old post cemetery at GPS 42.83827, -105.47836.

Jim Bridges (d. 1881) was a typical frontier badass. He got his kicks by pulling out his pistol just to scare people. One night at a boardinghouse in Fort Fetterman, Bridges and a fellow tenant argued over who'd get the last serving of mashed potatoes. As he often did, Bridges whipped out his gun to settle the argument—but his antagonist was slightly faster. He shot Bridges dead and presumably got seconds of mashed potatoes.

Bridges was buried in the military cemetery.

BULLDOZER RAMPAGE
Gillette

The bulldozer was left wedged inside an apartment building at 904 Church Ave., or GPS 44.286256, -105.481946.

Some deadly weapons are strange. Just before 3 a.m. on May 1, 1981, a drunken twenty-two-year-old electrician named John D. Thompson hijacked a forty-seven-ton Caterpillar D-9 bulldozer from a field behind a nightclub (GPS 44.290984, -105.488062). His seventy-five-minute rampage ran amok over twenty-four city blocks, smashing nineteen cars and parts of two apartment buildings, knocking down fences and power poles, cutting a gas line, ripping up yards, and ruining a half mile of paved road. Damage was estimated at $3 million.

Thompson bailed out of the bulldozer after a cop fired four shotgun blasts at him; the driverless bulldozer then plowed into another apartment building. Thompson later pleaded guilty to destruction of property and unauthorized use of a motor vehicle and was sentenced to three to ten years in prison.

Luckily, nobody was hurt in the berserk rampage, but it spawned a popular bumper sticker: "When we outlaw bulldozers, only outlaws will have bulldozers."

See also Bulldozer Rampage (Granby).

MOTHER DECAPITATES TODDLERS
Gillette
Mount Pisgah Cemetery is at 804 South Emerson Ave. The children's graves are at GPS 44.28433, -105.50054.

On April 25, 1989, in a meth-soaked psychotic episode, Laura Lee Rice decapitated her little daughters—fifteen-month-old Danielle and four-month-old JoAnn—and stuffed them in plastic trash bags because she believed they were "clones" of her real daughters. She claimed a mysterious visitor told her the only way she could get her children back was to kill the clones.

The corpses were found in Rice's trailer at the Hitching Post Trailer Court south of Gillette (GPS 44.23610, -105.46091). They were buried together.

Later that year after being charged with two counts of first-degree murder, Rice was found not guilty by reason of insanity and was sent to the state mental hospital in Evanston, where she has lived ever since. In recent years, doctors have sought more freedom for Rice, but it has been denied.

Doctors say Rice suffers from Capgras syndrome, a schizophrenic condition where one believes family members have been replaced by evil clones. Rice has often complained of sharp pains in her neck, chest, and stomach, which she believed were caused by the clones "taking bites out of her body with their eyes."

Fueled by meth and mental illness, Laura Lee Rice beheaded her two toddler girls in 1989, believing they were merely clones of her real children.

DEATH ON THE CLIFFS
Green River

The murder site is at the end of Lost Dog Road. To get there, drive seven and a half miles south from Green River on WY 530; Lost Dog Road cuts to the south and ends about ten miles later at the cliffs (GPS 41.297597, -109.548197).

Bob Duke and Liana Davidson were high school sweethearts who married right after high school because she was pregnant. It was an uneasy marriage, but everyone seemed to be making the best of it.

On August 10, 1996, during a Saturday afternoon outing on the remote Lost Dog Trail overlooking Flaming Gorge Reservoir, Liana and their five-year-old son, Erik, lost their footing and tumbled down a two-hundred-foot cliff, bouncing off rocky ledges before crashing to their deaths below. Rescuers cried as their bodies were winched up in a basket, Erik in his dead mother's arms.

A terrible accident, the police said. The widowed Bob Duke collected $60,000 in insurance money and moved away, but the little town of Green River wasn't done with him yet.

Three years after his wife and son were killed, a friend of Duke's came forward with a bizarre story. Duke, he said, had offered him $23,000 to kill Liana and Erik two weeks before they died. And Duke had recently asked the same friend to kill his parents, popular teachers in Green River.

Duke was arrested. At trial, prosecutors painted him as an ambitious killer who was in an unwanted marriage and didn't want to pay child support.

In 2001—five years after his wife and son's death—Duke was convicted on two counts of murder and four counts of soliciting murder. The judge sentenced him to six consecutive life terms, but he insisted it had been an accident.

"I am sorry that my grief did not meet the expectations of the public," he said as he was sentenced. "But my thoughts are my thoughts."

Bob Duke murdered wife Liana and her five-year-old son, Erik, by pushing them from the sheer Lost Dog Cliffs near Green River in 1996.

Liana Duke (1974–1996) and **Erik** (1991–1996) were buried at Green River's Riverview Cemetery, just north of I-80 on Cemetery Road. Their graves are in Section K, or GPS 41.53328, -109.45726.

ANDREW PIXLEY MURDERS
Jackson

The Wort Hotel is at 50 North Glenwood St., or GPS 43.479914, -110.76364.

Judge Robert McAuliffe had wanted to take his wife and three young daughters to Yellowstone for a long time, but on August 7, 1964, the Illinois family's dream vacation to Wyoming turned into a nightmare.

Around midnight, after a floor show in the Wort Hotel's downstairs lounge, the McAuliffes checked on their daughters, whom they'd left asleep in a second-floor room.

Judge McAuliffe was horrified to find the bloody bodies of little Debby, twelve, and Cindy, eight, half naked on the floor. They had been raped, strangled, and bludgeoned brutally with a large rock. Six-year-old sister Susan was unharmed in her bed.

Also lying on the floor in a stupor was the barefoot and blood-spattered Andrew Pixley, a twenty-year-old transient dishwasher. He'd sneaked into the room through an open window.

Transient dishwasher Andrew Pixley raped and slaughtered two young girls in a second-floor room in Jackson's Wort Hotel in 1964.

"My God, you've killed my daughters!" McAuliffe screamed as he held Pixley until police arrived.

Pixley, who claimed he was drunk and didn't remember the attack, was first jailed in Jackson, but when lynching rumors started circulating, he was moved among several jails.

After admitting he killed Cindy, Pixley was convicted by a jury in Deborah's murder and sentenced to die in Wyoming's gas chamber. He smiled when the order was read, causing a angry Judge McAuliffe to yell in court, "Laugh some more, you animal!"

Pixley wanted no appeals and even opposed one stay of execution, asking the governor to let him die.

He got his wish. A little after midnight on December 10, 1965, Pixley died fourteen seconds after lethal gas started spewing into the gas chamber in Rawlins. He was the first inmate to be executed by Wyoming in twenty years—and the last until the 1992 execution of killer Mark Hopkinson.

After he was pronounced dead, Pixley's eyes were removed and donated to the University of Colorado Medical School at his request. His body was returned to family in Dallas, Oregon.

Deborah and Cindy McAuliffe were buried in Maywood, Illinois. Relatives say Judge McAuliffe never fully recovered from the horror of his daughters' murder and died of a heart attack in 1998.

See also Wyoming Frontier Prison Museum (Rawlins) and Executed Killer Mark Hopkinson's Grave (Fort Bridger).

AMY BECHTEL DISAPPEARS
Lander

At 2:30 on the gray afternoon of July 24, 1997, a twenty-four-year-old long-distance runner named Amy Wroe Bechtel ducked into

Lander's Camera Connection on an errand on her way to jog near Loop Road in the Shoshone National Forest.

Then she vanished.

When Bechtel's husband of one year, Steve, came home around 4:30 p.m., their house was empty, but by 10:30 p.m. when she still hadn't come home, he called the sheriff and reported his wife missing. About 1 a.m., some of Bechtel's friends found her white Toyota station wagon parked on the south side of the intersection of Louis Lake Road and Burnt Gulch Road (GPS 42.678435, -108.875563), where she'd intended to run. (The spot is about two and a half miles south of Frye Lake.) Her keys, expensive sunglasses, and errand list were still in the car, but her wallet was missing.

By 3 a.m., in a constant rain, a major search was launched, and soon hundreds of volunteers, search dogs, horses, and helicopters were searching for Amy.

Searchers scoured caves, old cabins, mines, and culverts without luck. A print matching Amy's size-8 running shoes was found east of her parked car, but the print was inadvertently destroyed before police could analyze it.

Suspicion immediately fell on Steve Bechtel, but evidence was thin. On the advice of his lawyer, Steve refused to take a polygraph test, and without any other physical evidence, investigators were stymied. Amy's friends and family flooded Wyoming with posters; her story was featured in *People* magazine and the TV show *Unsolved Mysteries*—but no solid leads came.

In 2003, Steve remarried, and he still lives in the same house in Lander.

Some have suggested that Amy might have been abducted by presumed serial killer Dale Wayne Eaton, who was believed to be in the Lander area on the day Amy disappeared. He murdered Lisa

Marie Kimmell in the 1988 "Lil Miss" slaying but hadn't yet been identified at the time of Amy Wroe Bechtel's disappearance. Eaton, now on Wyoming's death row, has never spoken about it. The case remains open.

See also Lil Miss Murder (Casper).

MATTHEW SHEPARD MURDER
Laramie

The site where Shepard was found is beside an isolated dirt road east of Laramie at GPS 41.30224, -105.51763. A pile of stones shaped like an arrow marks the spot.

The Equality State was thrust into the unwelcome glare of national attention on October 8, 1998, when University of Wyoming student Matthew Shepard, a five-foot-two, 102-pound kid who happened to be gay, met two local thugs at the off-campus Fireside Lounge, 201 East Custer St. (GPS 41.309312, -105.594729).

The thugs—Aaron McKinney, twenty-two, and Russell Henderson, twenty-one—pretended to be gay and drank with Shepard before offering him a ride home. In the truck, McKinney whipped out a .357 pistol. "Guess what," he said. "We're not gay. And you're gonna get jacked."

They stole Shepard's wallet and drove him to a remote spot more than a mile from town, where they pistol-whipped him and beat him with their fists mercilessly. They then tied his beaten body to a split-rail fence, beat him some more, took his shoes, and left him to die in near-freezing temperatures.

Eighteen hours later, a cyclist found Shepard, still alive but bleeding profusely and struggling to breathe. His face was caked with blood, but his tears had washed streaks down his cheeks. He never regained consciousness. The damage to his brain stem and skull was so severe that doctors were unable to operate, and

Gay college student Matthew Shepard was brutally beaten by two local thugs and left to die on this buckrail fence in 1998.

Shepard died just past midnight on October 12, 1998, in a Colorado hospital.

Shepard's funeral at St. Mark's Episcopal Church, 701 South Wolcott St. in Casper (GPS 42.843521, -106.323817), attracted an overflow crowd and national media—and the homophobic flock of

Rev. Fred Phelps's Westboro Baptist Church of Topeka, Kansas, who created a furor by carrying picket signs saying, GOD HATES FAGS and FAGS BURN IN HELL.

Shepard's body was cremated and his ashes given to his family.

In 1999, Henderson cut a deal with prosecutors to describe the killing in exchange for two life sentences without the possibility of parole. A jury later convicted McKinney, but while they considered the death penalty, Shepard's parents approved a deal to give him two sentences of life without parole. "We are giving him life in the memory of one who no longer lives," they said. Both killers remain in prison.

The horrific murder energized the movement to create hate-crime protection for gays.

The crime was explored by Judy Shepard, Matthew's mother, in her 2009 book *The Meaning of Matthew* and in film and stage versions of *The Laramie Project*. Singer Melissa Etheridge's 1999 song "Scarecrow" is a tribute to Shepard.

The Matthew Shepard Foundation is at 4010 South Poplar in Casper (www.matthewshepard.org).

TRAIN ROBBER'S CAMPGROUND
Laramie

The campground was on the south side of Grand Avenue about seven tenths of a mile east of the Ivinson Home for Aged Ladies, or GPS 41.30850, -105.55499.

Despite the fact that he never got rich robbing trains, **Bill Carlisle** (1890–1964) was one of the most popular—and longest lived—bandits of the Old West. And for a time in his later years, he owned the popular Spring Creek Campground in Laramie, a favorite stop during the rise of the car culture in the 1940s and 1950s. It offered red sandstone cabins and places to camp under the stars—and a chance to meet the last of Wyoming's old-fashioned train bandits.

After wrecking one train, he reportedly held up passengers with a candy-filled glass pistol. After another robbery, he sent a telegram to the Union Pacific, thanking them for the loot. In the 1940s—after getting out of prison—he toured as a promoter for Hollywood Westerns. Once, he even stopped at the Union Pacific Museum in Omaha to confirm that a gun they displayed was, indeed, the one he used in the hold-up.

In 1946, he wrote a book, *Bill Carlisle: Lone Bandit,* illustrated by famous artist Charles M. Russell. Today, only 177 original copies are known to exist.

Carlisle is buried in Coatesville, Pennsylvania.

VIGILANTES 4, SCOUNDRELS 0
Laramie

The Belle of the West Saloon faced the railroad tracks from the northeast corner of South First Street and East Garfield Avenue, or GPS 41.310299, -105.596069.

By the time Laramie had become an official town in 1868, the Belle of the West tent saloon and dance hall was a thriving den of thieves and rowdies—so violent that the locals called it the "Bucket of Blood." So it was a natural "town hall" for self-appointed mayor Ace Moore, a local heavy who quickly hired five thugs as his "marshals." They held trials in the saloon's back rooms, often stealing everything from well-to-do travelers who got off the train—or garroting anybody they deemed a threat to their interests.

But on October 29, 1868, the local citizenry had had enough of Moore's iron-fisted government. Some five hundred armed vigilantes launched a coordinated attack on several outlaw hangouts, including the Belle of the West. Most of the townfolk were embroiled in the chaotic gun battle, where five men were killed and fifteen wounded.

Moore and three of his henchmen surrendered, but they got no mercy. The vigilantes hanged three of them—including Moore—behind the Frontier Hotel, which sat beside the train tracks at the western end of East Ivinson Avenue (GPS 41.312144, -105.596343). The fourth was hanged elsewhere.

The four outlaws' corpses were piled in a wagon and dumped in an unmarked mass grave somewhere outside the city limits. It has never been found.

The Belle of the West continued to be a gathering place for Laramie. In 1870, it hosted the first Wyoming trial in which women sat on the jury.

GUNSLINGER UNDER A MICROSCOPE
Laramie

The University of Wyoming's Anthropology Building is at 12th and Lewis Streets on the campus, or GPS 41.315238, -105.581167. Access is limited to students and researchers.

Notorious badman **Cy Williams** (c. 1833–1868) operated a roadhouse near Fort Laramie, where travelers could get a bed, a meal, and lots of liquor. He'd killed at least two men in his career as a gunslinger. After one deadly gunfight with some Indian teens, Williams himself was shot dead and buried on the spot on a remote ranch.

In 1980, an excavator unearthed Williams's body, which was identified by forensic anthropologists and archaeologists using three nineteenth-century nickels in the corpse's pocket, a silver wedding band and a black rubber mourning ring on one finger, diaries by a local rancher—oh, and a .44- or .45-caliber bullet wound in the torso and a shot to the head.

Today, Cy Williams is doing more good in death than he ever did in life. His body—kept in the Human Remains Repository at UW—is studied by anthropology and pre-med students.

LARAMIE JAIL
Laramie
The jail no longer exists but sat on the south side of East Ivinson Avenue between Second and Third Streets, at GPS 41.311911, -105.593972.

In its heyday, the Laramie jail was a busy place.

In 1876, not long after he'd shot the famous Wild Bill Hickok in Deadwood, South Dakota, Jack McCall was in a Laramie bar boasting about the murder. A deputy U.S. marshal sitting nearby immediately arrested him and tossed him in the Laramie jail. While he was awaiting extradition to the Dakota Territory, McCall admitted to a newspaper reporter that he'd killed Hickok because Hickok had killed his brother. McCall was eventually sent back to face a trial, where he was convicted and hanged.

Another Deadwood character, Calamity Jane Canary, also spent some time in the Laramie jail for disturbing the peace.

In 1877, several suspects in a nearby stagecoach robbery cooled their heels in the jail until local authorities decided they didn't have enough evidence to charge them. They were released and quickly left Laramie before anybody realized the gang leader was Jesse James.

RAPIST DOCTOR'S CLINIC
Lovell
"Doc" John Story practiced at 25 West 10th St., or GPS 44.828074, -108.394005.

Half the 2,500 people in little Lovell are Mormon, a religion in which women consider themselves property of men or the Church. Dr. John Story—a pillar in the local Baptist church—opened his practice in Lovell in 1958 and was widely respected … by most.

By the late 1960s, rumors started circulating about "Doc." Women with ailments such as infected ear lobes and sore feet were routinely subjected to long, painful pelvic exams. Some even said it felt a lot like sex. The rumors split the community down the middle.

In 1985, Story was charged with nine rape counts for assaults that reportedly happened at his clinic between 1967 and 1977. Although many women refused to go public for fear of repercussions from neighbors, Story was convicted on six counts, ranging from a minimum of ten years for a count of second-degree sexual assault to a maximum of twenty years for two counts of first-degree rape.

Story served sixteen years in prison. He was paroled in 2001 and moved to another state.

The case is detailed in Jack Olsen's classic 1989 true-crime saga, *Doc*.

THE LUSTY MADAMS OF LUSK
Lusk

A famous Wyoming bumper sticker proclaims: "Don't tell my mother I work in the oilfield. She thinks I'm a piano player in a whorehouse."

After madam Dell Burke died in 1980, her bordello—the Yellow Hotel—fell into disrepair but still stands.

For a long time, there might have been more whorehouses than pianos in wild and woolly Wyoming, where winters are long and cold. And two of the most famous madams in Wyoming's long hooker history made the winter nights around the little farm town of Lusk a little warmer.

About the time Custer was being massacred in Montana, a red-haired strumpet known only as **Mother Featherlegs** (d. 1879) opened a brothel on the Cheyenne–Black Hills trail south of modern-day Lusk. Nobody knew the middle-aged madam's real name, but her nickname—derived from her habit of hiking up her skirts while riding a horse, exposing her lacy bloomers—was much more colorful anyway.

Mother Featherlegs' bawdy house did brisk business with the outlaws, cowboys, and gamblers traveling between Cheyenne and Deadwood. Highwaymen along the trail often asked Mother Featherlegs to hold their stolen booty until they could safely turn it into cash—which they likely spent at her whorehouse.

Among her admirers was a ne'er-do-well trapper named "Dangerous Dick" Davis, who lived with the madam.

Then one day in 1879, Mother Featherlegs' murdered body was found beside a nearby spring, and Dangerous Dick had disappeared along with her cash and jewelry. Just before vigilantes lynched Dangerous Dick in Louisiana, he confessed to killing Mother Featherlegs—whose real name was Charlotte Shepard, a woman who'd once run with a gang of bayou thieves.

Mother Featherlegs was buried on the spot. In 1964, some locals decided to mark her grave with a 3,500-pound red granite marker, in an event attended by hundreds of people. Today Mother Featherlegs' grave is about ten miles south of Lusk on the east side of the Old Cheyenne Trail (Silver Springs Road), or GPS 42.626124, -104.531243. This is a very rough road, so don't even try to traverse it without four-wheel drive in dry weather.

One of the contributors to the madam's monument was **Dell Burke** (1888–1980), operator of Lusk's famous Yellow Hotel, one of the most renowned brothels in Wyoming.

Across from the train depot, Dell's two-story hotel at 208 West Griffith (GPS 42.765244, -104.453963) had become a popular stop for travelers after she swept into town with the 1919 oil boom. In time, she even erected billboards touting her "services," which included juicy steaks, pretty girls, gambling, and lots of booze.

In 1929, eager to thwart frequent raids of her business, Dell loaned the City of Lusk money to buy equipment for the town's light and power plant. So the next time some moralizing prosecutor threatened to shut her down, Dell reminded the city fathers that she could literally turn out their lights—and the raids stopped.

Over the years, Dell Burke became one of the leading citizens of Lusk, even serving as an ex officio member of the chamber of commerce and donating generously to many local charities.

In 1980, when Dell died at age ninety-two, she left an estate valued at $1.3 million. Her body was cremated, and her hotel and its contents were auctioned off. Today the hotel is abandoned and decaying but still standing.

OWEN WISTER COUNTRY
Medicine Bow

The Virginian Hotel is at 404 US 30, or GPS 41.895811, -106.20058. Other Wister-related sites are nearby.

After an 1885 trip to the railroad town of Medicine Bow, author Owen Wister knew he'd found the perfect setting for a great cowboy novel. So when his seminal western *The Virginian* was published in 1902, Medicine Bow became famous. It's here that gunslinger Trampas calls a Southern stranger a "son of a bitch," to which the tall, dark Virginian responds famously, "When you call me that—smile."

At the book's climax, the Virginian guns down Trampas in front of Buffalo's Occidental Hotel (10 North Main St., or GPS 44.347057, -106.699208) in Western literature's first classic gunfight.

But the real town of Medicine Bow still has plenty of Wister history.

When Wister arrived late one night in 1885, he couldn't find a room, so he slept on the counter of the General Store, a scene that also found its way into the book. (He was traveling with rancher Frank Wolcott, a blubbery old Army officer who later led the ill-fated invasion of Johnson County.)

Wister returned many times to Wyoming, and especially to Medicine Bow, to hang out with all the colorful cowboys, Indians, and frontier characters who filled his stories.

The original General Store is preserved on the south side of the railroad tracks at GPS 41.89465, -106.20116.

A night spent on the counter of the Medicine Bow General Store led Owen Wister to write the seminal western novel, The Virginian.

In 1939, a petrified-wood monument to Wister was erected beside the small museum across the highway from the hotel. In 1970, Wister's Jackson-area log cabin was also relocated to Medicine Bow. Both stand beside the museum at GPS 41.89544, -106.20007.

On the north side of the tracks, the Virginian Hotel broke ground in 1901—the year before Wister's novel of the same name—and was finished in 1911. The three-and-a-half-story Renaissance Revival building was built with concrete blocks made from sand dredged from the Medicine Bow River. When it opened, it contained the first electric lights and sewer in town, but that's where time stood still ... today none of its rooms have telephones or televisions.

But it's possible to see bullet holes in the walls of the Owen Wister Saloon downstairs, where a few real gunslingers have obviously been hanging out.

Wister died in 1938 and is buried in Philadelphia's Laurel Hill Cemetery.

See also the Occidental Hotel and Johnson County War (Buffalo).

GAME WARDENS MURDERED
Medicine Bow National Forest
The murder site is deep inside rugged wilderness at GPS 41.286303, -107.162801. Do not visit without an experienced guide, a reliable four-wheel-drive vehicle, sturdy hiking shoes, and adequate survival preparation.

Prospector and poacher **John Malten** (1888–1945) was a former sharpshooter in the Kaiser's army in World War I, and he lived in a cabin deep in the wilderness of Wyoming's Sierra Madre Mountains.

In 1943, Malten served more than nine months in jail after game wardens Don Simpson and Bill Lakanen found him with illegal beaver pelts. When he got out, Malten promised he'd never do jail time again—and he'd kill any warden who came near his Nugget Gulch cabin.

On October 31, 1945, he made good on his promise. When Simpson and Lakanen came back to check on Malten, he ambushed them. Lakanen was shot in the head before he even got out of his truck, and Simpson was wounded before fleeing into the timber, where Malten found him and shot him dead with one of the wardens' .38 handgun.

Malten tried to set fire to the corpses, but instead his cabin caught fire. Two days later, searchers found the wardens' unburned bodies and charred bones in the cabin's ashes. They believe Malten died in the fire, and he was never seen again, but his death was never confirmed. Some even believe Malten escaped and other wardens burned his cabin to cover up their comrades' missteps. Either way, a warrant was issued for Malten's arrest twenty-two days after the killing, and it has never been served.

Don Simpson (1906–1945) was buried in the Saratoga Cemetery, a half mile east of town on Cemetery Road, at GPS 41.45861,

The rusted hulk of a pickup truck is all that remains at the spot where a mad trapper murdered two game wardens in 1945.
Roderick Laird & Mike Martell

-106.79450. **Bill Lakanen** (1901–1945) was buried at the Rawlins Cemetery, 915 Third St. His grave is on the western edge of the cemetery, at GPS 41.79569, -107.24017. Both are honored on the Wyoming Peace Officers Memorial Wall in Douglas, where eight of Wyoming's fifty-nine fallen lawmen are game wardens.

Today some ashy ground still remains at the site, along with the rusted hulk of the wardens' abandoned pickup truck—left where it sat during the murder—with a tree now growing through its passenger compartment. Of all the sites in this book, this one is least accessible. After jouncing over a miles of unmaintained, primitive forest roads that require four-wheel drive in the best weather, you must hike through rugged terrain and dense forest to the site. It's an all-day expedition from the nearest civilization.

Simpson's badge—still bearing a bullet hole—is part of a Wyoming Game & Fish memorial to the slain wardens being planned in Casper.

Some artifacts of this killing—including Malten's murder weapon and a melted aspirin bottle containing gold nuggets that Malten had picked up—are displayed at the Saratoga Museum, 104 Constitution Ave. (GPS 41.44486, -106.80679). Summer hours daily 1–4. Free admission. www.saratoga-museum.com.

TEAPOT DOME
Midwest area

Teapot Rock, the rocky outcropping for which the oil-rich area was named, is about thirty miles north of Casper, or GPS 43.232984, -106.311189. To get there, drive north from Casper on I-25 to WY 259; the rock is about four miles from the exit.

This seventy-five-foot sandstone mimetolith—a rock formation resembling a person, animals, or other object—once reminded settlers of a giant teapot until a storm knocked over the "handle" in 1962. But by then, Teapot Rock had already become a potent symbol of government corruption and greed.

Although it has lost its "handle," Teapot Rock still stands as a symbol of political corruption in America.

When oil was discovered in the area in the early 1900s, the rock lent its name to the Teapot Dome, a rich oilfield under federal land that the government had designated as an emergency oil reserve for the U.S. Navy. Many oil companies were chagrined, believing they could supply any oil the government needed—for a profit, of course.

Among the politicians who wanted to open the field to oil companies was New Mexico Senator Albert B. Fall (1861–1944), a lawyer who'd successfully defended the accused killer of famous Sheriff Pat Garrett. Soon after President Warren G. Harding appointed Fall as his Secretary of the Interior in 1921, Fall took control of the Teapot Dome oilfields and leased them to Harry Sinclair's Mammoth Oil Company.

Ah, but in politics, no good deed goes unrewarded. Grateful oilmen showered Fall with "gifts" and "loans" amounting to about

$400,000. He kept these "gifts" secret, but Washington insiders noticed Fall was enjoying a lifestyle well beyond his means.

The scandal finally broke in 1924. It was just one more blow to the public trust, which had been rocked just a few years before by baseball's Black Sox scandal—and it gave us a new slang term: "fall guy." It was Enron and Watergate combined. Fall was convicted, fined $100,000, and imprisoned for a year—the first American Cabinet secretary ever to go to prison for misconduct in office. Disgraced and impoverished, he died in his sleep four days after his eighty-third birthday. He is buried in Evergreen Alameda Cemetery, 4371 Alameda Ave. in El Paso, Texas. His grave is in Section K, Lot 211, Space 2, or GPS 31.77337, -106.44018.

Teapot Rock was listed on the National Register of Historic Places in 1974.

LYNCHING OF DIAMOND L. SLIM
Newcastle

A historical marker exists on the northwest corner of West Main Street and North Railway Avenue at GPS 43.85433, -104.20589.

Some say Diamond L. Slim Clifton (1872–1903) had a crush on the pretty Louella Church, who rebuffed him. Others say he felt cheated in a business deal with Louella's husband, John. But after Clifton murdered the popular young couple, nobody waited around to hear the true story.

Impatient with the pace of justice, vigilantes raided the jail and took Clifton a few blocks to a nearby railroad trestle, where they looped a noose around his neck and pushed him off the edge.

Unfortunately (for Slim), the rope was too long and the drop too far. The force of his body hitting the end of the rope decapitated him.

Whether the local mortician had a macabre sense of humor or was making a social comment, we cannot know, but he sewed Slim's head back on his torso backward. He then displayed the re-combobulated cadaver in his front window for people to see. "Even women who could never stand the sight of blood were among the viewers," the local newspaper said.

Diamond L. Slim was eventually buried in an unmarked grave at Newcastle's Greenwood Cemetery, and the spot has been lost over the years.

The Anna Miller Museum at 401 Delaware (GPS 43.84991, -104.19304) has a display devoted to the lynching of Diamond L. Slim. The museum is open during summer, Mon–Fri 9–5 and Sat 9–noon; free admission.

DEPUTY ARTHUR OSBORN'S GRAVE
Pine Bluffs

Pine Bluffs Cemetery is a quarter mile south of I-80 on Beech Avenue. The grave is in Lot 35, Block 3 of the original cemetery, or GPS 41.17241, -104.06253.

Veteran Deputy Arthur Osborn (1882–1927) didn't know it was the infamous gangster Herman Barker—favorite son of "bloody mama" Ma Barker and brother of public enemies Doc, Fred, and Lloyd Barker—who cashed some stolen bank bonds at the American National Bank in Cheyenne (1602 Capitol Ave., or GPS 41.13280, -104.81545). But he set up a roadblock about five miles west of tiny Pine Bluffs to catch the thief.

He flagged down the car and walked up, but Barker snatched a gun from the seat beside him and shot Osborn twice, killing him.

Barker was never brought to justice. A few weeks later, he killed himself during a gunfight with Tulsa cops. His role in Deputy Osborn's death came out only when a female companion who'd been in the car was arrested later and told investigators about the murder.

See also Gangster Lloyd Barker's Grave (Brighton).

EARL DURAND'S RAMPAGE
Powell

The former First National Bank and death site are at 101 North Bent St., or GPS 44.752912, -108.75768.

Mountain man **Earl Durand** (1913–1939) was rumored to be a shaggy, raw-meat-eating wild man who pitched a tent behind his parents' home when he wasn't living in the wilderness for weeks at a time. The eighth-grade dropout was a crack shot who ran miles every day, long before jogging was fashionable.

One night in March 1939, Durand and some friends poached four elk and were arrested. Durand got six months in the Cody jail and a $100 fine, but later that day, Durand clocked his jailer with a milk bottle, took him hostage, and escaped.

Deputy D. M. Baker and Powell Marshal Chuck Lewis tracked Durand to his parents' ranch house, but Durand fatally shot them both as they approached (although his hostage escaped in the chaos).

For nearly a week, Durand eluded the posse in the mountains. He even left them a note: "Of course I know that I'm done for and when you kill me I suggest you have my head mounted and hang it up in the courthouse for the sake of law and order. Your beloved

When free-spirited young mountain man Earl Durand was arrested for poaching elk, he exploded in a deadly rampage that left six people dead.

enemy, Earl Durand." The return address: Earl Durand, Undertaker's Office, Powell, Wyoming.

Montana National Guardsmen were called out, and Wyoming sent howitzers and mortars to support the search for the "Tarzan of the Tetons."

Deputy Arthur Argento and civilian Orville Linaberry were killed approaching a mountain fortress where Durand was spotted, and the posse fled, leaving their bodies on the mountain and telling a reporter, "We haven't got him cornered. He's got us cornered."

Durand escaped again. He hijacked a car and left the owners standing on the roadside. "Come to my funeral, boys!" he shouted as he drove off.

On March 24, he strode into Powell's First National Bank with a .30-.30 rifle, a pistol, and a backpack. He announced he was robbing the bank and took up to $3,000. Inexplicably, he opened fire, blasting away at walls, windows, and nearby businesses for nearly ten minutes while lawmen were gathered forty miles away looking for him.

High school junior Tipton Cox, who was skipping school, was across First Street at the Powell Texaco station (now a restaurant at 113 South Bent St., or GPS 44.75266, -108.757659). The station owner gave him a rifle as Durand left the bank with a phalanx of hostages, including teller Johnny Gawthrop. Suddenly, citizens opened fire, and Gawthrop fell mortally wounded, exposing Durand. Young Tipton Cox fired a single shot, wounding Durand. (At the time, the bank's main door opened onto First Street, but it has since been moved to the Bent Street side.)

Durand crawled back into the bank and shot himself. Just to be sure, the bank president picked up Durand's rifle and shot his corpse once in the head.

The Durand rampage became a national media sensation. So many people wanted to see Durand's body at Easton's Funeral Home (111 West Third St., or GPS 44.755556, -108.759444) that the morticians laid him on a couch in the foyer so gawkers could file past.

A wounded Earl Durand shot himself just inside the door (now gone) in this Powell bank building.

To this day, Durand has his supporters in Powell. Many of them say he supplied poached meat to poor, Depression-era neighbors, and that he was hectored by local cops to the breaking point.

Durand was buried privately at Powell's Crown Hill Cemetery, 678 Lane 9. His grave is in Block 13, Lot 29, or GPS 44.75229, -108.71401.

Lawmen **D. M. Baker** (1868–1939) and **Chuck Lewis** (1895–1939) are also buried in Crown Hill. Baker is in Block 14, Lot 21, or GPS 44.75233, -108.71178, and Lewis is in Block 20, Lot 3, or GPS 44.75206, -108.06271.

Arthur Argento (1893–1939) is buried in the Meeteetse Cemetery at Block 17, Lot 4, or GPS 44.15008, -108.86332. **Orville Linaberry** (1897–1939) is buried somewhere in Cody's Riverside Cemetery, 1721 Gulch St., but the exact location has been lost. All four are honored on the Fallen Officers Memorial in Douglas (GPS 42.76839, -105.408631). In addition, the Powell police headquarters (250 North Clark St., or GPS 44.75499, -108.75641) was renamed in 2007 for Chuck Lewis.

Slain hostage **John Gawthrop** (1919–1939) is buried in Cody's Riverside Cemetery, Section 5, Block 3D, or GPS 44.51857, -109.08221.

Tipton Cox (1922–2006) died in a Cody nursing home at age eighty-four. Always a hero, he was a Marine pilot during World War II in the Pacific, and one of two pilots who rescued sixteen scientists on Eniwetok Atoll after the atomic bomb test in the Pacific, for which he earned an Air Medal. His grave is in Cody's Riverside Cemetery, Section 15, Block 60E, or GPS 44.52023, -109.08374.

Today Durand's rifle is displayed along with many other artifacts at Powell's Homesteader Museum, 324 East First St., at GPS 44.75269, -108.75564. Summer hours are Tue–Fri 10–5 and Sat 10–2; off-season hours vary. Free admission; www.homesteadermuseum.com.

The Durand case was explored in Dr. Jerred Metz's 2005 book *The Last Eleven Days of Earl Durand.* The rampage was also made into a highly fictionalized 1974 film starring Martin Sheen and Slim Pickens called *The Legend of Earl Durand.*

BIG NOSE GEORGE BECOMES A PAIR OF SHOES
Rawlins

The Carbon County Museum is at 904 West Walnut St., or GPS 41.79116, -107.24716. It is open (June–September) Tues–Fri 10 a.m. –6 p.m. and Sat 1–5 p.m.; (October–May) Tues–Sat 1–5 p.m. Free admission; www.carboncountymuseum.org.

Rustler and would-be train robber **George Parrott** (d. 1881) had an enormous nose, earning him his nickname. And in death, this

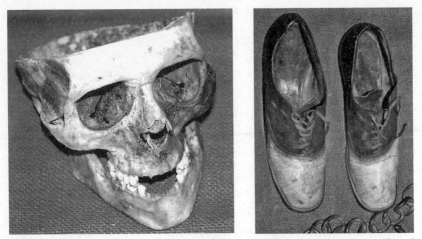

After his lynching "Big Nose" George Parrott was dissected by a local doctor who used his body parts for various macabre purposes. His skull cap became an ashtray; his skin became a pair of shoes.

small-time crook also became one of Wyoming's biggest outlaw legends.

In 1878, Big Nose George and his gang planned to derail a Union Pacific train near Medicine Bow and rob it. But they were discovered by a section crew before the train passed, and soon a sheriff's posse was hot on their trail.

Cornered in Rattlesnake Canyon near Elk Mountain, the gang killed two deputies and scattered.

A couple years later, Big Nose George got drunk in Montana and spilled the beans about the robbery and murder. He was quickly arrested and brought back to Rawlins to stand trial, but vigilantes stopped the train along the way and grabbed George, intending to lynch him. George pleaded for his life and promised to tell the whole story if he was allowed to live. The mob let him go.

George was convicted of murder and sentenced to hang, but he wasn't going quietly. During an escape attempt a few weeks before his execution date, he cracked the skull of a jailer and might have gotten away if the jailer's wife hadn't pulled a gun on the outlaw.

The locals decided George had overstayed his welcome. On March 22, 1881, a mob of masked men snatched George from his cell and strung him up on a telegraph pole next to the railroad tracks near Front and Third Streets (GPS 41.78708,-107.237694).

After the corpse swung in the Wyoming wind for a few hours, two local doctors claimed it. They intended to dissect Big Nose George in an attempt to understand his criminal behavior.

Robert Widdowfield was one of two deputies killed by "Big Nose" George Parrott's gang in 1878 and was buried in the now-secluded Old Carbon Cemetery near Medicine Bow.

Drs. Thomas Maghee and John Osborne, with the help of a fifteen-year-old assistant named Lillian Heath, removed Parrott's brain but found nothing unusual.

And that's where things get weird.

First, Osborne made a plaster death mask of George (his ears didn't appear because they were torn off when the noose was violently thrown around his neck before he was hanged). He then flensed the skin from the outlaw's chest and thighs and sent it to a Denver tannery with instructions to make a medical bag and shoes from it—and he especially wanted George's nipples to decorate the shoes (they didn't). In a final insult, a small coin purse was made from the outlaw's scrotum.

Osborne kept the rest of George's dismembered body in a salt-filled whiskey barrel for about a year, occasionally experimenting on it. When he was done, he buried the barrel with its macabre contents in Dr. Maghee's backyard.

But he kept George's skull cap, which he later gave to Lillian Heath, who was to become Wyoming's first female doctor. She kept it as an ashtray and doorstop in her office.

In the meantime, Dr. Osborne got involved in politics. In 1892, he was elected governor of Wyoming. For his inauguration, he wore the shoes made from Big Nose George's skin.

Then in 1950, startled construction workers unearthed a grisly barrel full of human remains. They were identified as Big Nose George Parrott when Lillian Heath's skull cap fit the sawed-off skull perfectly. Except for the skull, the rest of Parrott's remains were buried at a secret location that's never been divulged.

Now the Carbon County Museum permanently (and proudly) displays George's death mask and capless skull beside Dr. Osborne's macabre shoes, along with other items related to the criminal.

The skull cap, medical bag, and the shackles George wore to his lynching are in the Union Pacific Railroad Museum, 200 Pearl St. in Council Bluffs, Iowa. The coin purse is missing.

Dr. John Osborne (1858–1943) is buried at Cedar Hill Cemetery in Princeton, Kentucky. **Dr. Lillian Heath** (1865–1962) is buried in the Rawlins Cemetery, 915 Third St.; her grave is in Section 10, Block 4, or GPS 41.79867, -107.23958.

The two lawmen killed by Parrott's gang were the first Wyoming officers killed in the line of duty. They are both honored among fallen lawmen at the Wyoming Peace Officers Memorial, 1556 Riverbend Dr. in Douglas (GPS 42.76839, -105.408631).

Deputy **Robert Widdowfield** (1846–1878) is buried at Old Carbon Cemetery, in the ghost town of Carbon, about fourteen miles west of Medicine Bow; his grave is at GPS 41.85223, -106.37901. Be forewarned: You'll probably need a four-wheel-drive vehicle to get there.

Railroad detective **Henry "Tip" Vincents** (1838–1878) is buried at Rawlins Cemetery, GPS 41.79826, -107.23859. Don't be confused: Because they died together, the citizens of Carbon County erected two stones to these two lawmen in Rawlins; however, Widdowfield's actual grave is in Old Carbon.

WYOMING FRONTIER PRISON MUSEUM
Rawlins
The historic prison is at 500 West Walnut, or GPS 41.792703, -107.242795. Summer hours are 8–5 seven days a week; off-season hours are Mon–Thurs 10:30 a.m.–1:30 p.m. Tours are offered. Admission is charged; www.wyomingfrontierprison.org.

Opened in 1901, this imposing and austere fortress was Wyoming's first state penitentiary. It had no electricity or running water, and it was so poorly heated that frigid temperatures were considered part of the punishment.

In the prison's eighty years, some 13,500 people lived there. Among its unique features was a dungeon, several different creepy versions of solitary confinement, and a "punishment pole" where

From 1901 to 1981, the cold and gothic Wyoming Frontier Prison housed the state's worst criminals. Today it's a museum.

handcuffed inmates were whipped with rubber hoses—a practice outlawed in 1930.

In 1916, the prison added the "death house," where executions were carried out. At first they used the unique Julien gallows on which Tom Horn was hanged in Cheyenne in 1903. In 1937, a gas chamber was installed. All together, fourteen men died in the frontier prison's death house (nine by hanging and five by gas).

The prison closed in 1981 and sat vacant until 1987, when it became a museum. Today it offers tours, the Wyoming Peace

Officers Museum, and a gift shop where visitors can buy inmate-made goods and other items.

And if you like ghost stories, this is a favorite hangout for paranormal investigators.

WYOMING STATE PENITENTIARY CEMETERY
Rawlins

The old cemetery is on the northeast side of the Wyoming Frontier Prison, 500 West Walnut, or GPS 41.795318, -107.240714.

Most cemeteries contain fascinating stories, but only in a prison cemetery do most of them have unhappy endings.

In the dozens of graves here are killers, con men, hucksters, and other unsavory sorts who died in prison and were never claimed by loved ones. In the end, they only got a cheap pine box and a concrete marker in a pauper's field beside the prison. Among the men buried here are:

- **Talton Taylor** (1898–1933), a Sheridan cowboy who killed a homesteader, was the last man executed by hanging in Wyoming (GPS 41.79550, -107.24084).

- **Paul Carroll** (1899–1937), assassin of a Union Pacific Railroad superintendent, was the first to die in Wyoming's new gas chamber. Luckily for him, the newfangled device was tested on live pigs before he went in (GPS 41.79518, -107.24068).

- **Henry Ruhl** (1909–1945), a triple killer, was the only federal execution in Wyoming history. In his final statement before entering the gas chamber he promised to "meet all law officers in Hell and talk it over" (GPS 41.79518, -107.24088).

- **Joseph Seng** (1882–1912) killed a man in a barroom brawl and was said to be an excellent catcher on the prison baseball team. He was hanged on the prison's high-tech gallows—recently moved to Rawlins from Cheyenne after the hanging of outlaw Tom Horn—which used a trapdoor, water buckets, counterweights, ropes, and pulleys that are set in motion when the condemned man steps onto the platform, essentially hanging himself. After Seng's death, the baseball team was never quite as good (GPS 41.79548, -107.24073).

- **Cleveland Brown Jr.** (1917–1945), who killed an elderly Kemmerer woman, was the third to die in the gas chamber (GPS 41.79533, -107.24091).

- **Frank Gimlin** (1915–1932), a car thief, was only sixteen when he hanged himself in his cell, becoming the youngest man ever to die in a Wyoming prison (GPS 41.79532, -107.24084).

- **Al Biscaro** (1885–1921) was a career criminal doing hard time when he used a smuggled gun to abduct two prison workers for a grand escape in a stolen car. When guards eventually caught up to him, he released his hostages and shot himself in the chest and head. His wife confessed to giving Biscaro the gun and as she stood over his corpse, she proclaimed, "Well, Old Scout, guess I will finish your sentence" (GPS 41.79551, -107.24072).

- **Jim Best** is the oldest inmate buried here. He was eighty-nine years old when he was given a new suit and $15 and released from prison in 1963. Best reportedly sat down on the front lawn for a while—then knocked on the front door to be readmitted. He died soon after (GPS 41.79523, -107.24066).

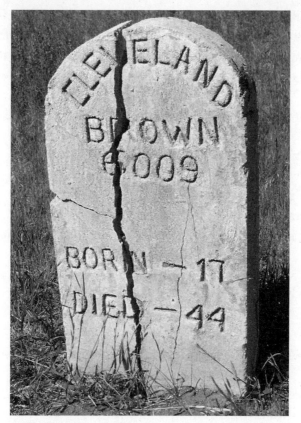

Killer Cleveland Brown was just twenty-eight when he became the third to die in Wyoming's gas chamber in 1945. Nobody claimed his body.

RODEO MURDERS
Rawlins

The Carbon County Fairgrounds are at 607 Rodeo St., or GPS 41.794636, -107.228794.

In the hot summer of 1974, four young girls disappeared over a two-month period—three of them from events at the Rawlins fairgrounds. The city was suddenly in a panic.

On July 4, 1974, Christy Gross of South Dakota and her friend Carlene Brown of Rawlins, both nineteen, disappeared from a Little Britches Rodeo. Gross's bludgeoned skeleton was found nine years later in a desolate area three miles north of Sinclair; Brown is still missing.

On August 4, fifteen-year-old Debra Meyer vanished while walking to the local movie theater. And nineteen days later, ten-year-old Jaylene Banker disappeared when she got separated from her friends at the county rodeo. Neither girl has ever been found.

The best suspect was a carnival worker and trucker named Royal Russell Long, who lived in Rawlins in 1974. But without bodies, charges were never filed. In 1985, Long got two life sentences for an unrelated Cheyenne kidnapping case in which another young girl went missing. He died of a heart attack in prison in 1993.

INFAMOUS LAWMAN ED CANTRELL'S GRAVE
Rock Springs
Rest Haven Memorial Gardens are at 250 Yellowstone Rd. The grave is at GPS 41.65054, -109.26022.

His fame as a quick-draw artist and one-time Wyoming cattle detective naturally invited comparisons between **Ed Cantrell** (1927–2004) and the legendary Tom Horn. And it was Cantrell's Wild West reputation that landed him in the unwelcome national spotlight.

In 1978, Cantrell was the public safety director in the rough-and-tumble boomtown of Rock Springs. One hot summer night, Cantrell, two officers, and an undercover drug agent named Michael Rosa were parked in an unmarked squad car outside a Rock Springs nightclub, the Silver Dollar Bar (now a motel at 1635 Elk St., or GPS 41.611315, -109.230537). Suddenly, Cantrell whipped out his pistol and shot Rosa between the eyes, killing him instantly.

214

A modern-day version of Tom Horn, Ed Cantrell was acquitted in the killing of an undercover narcotics agent in Rock Springs in 1978.

National media swooped down to cover this frontier-style gunfight in modern Wyoming between an old-fashioned cowboy cop and a long-haired New York–born undercover cop. The TV show *60 Minutes* aired two segments, and articles appeared in every newspaper and magazine from the *New York Times* to *People.*

Cantrell later testified he thought Rosa was reaching for a hidden gun when he shot him; prosecutors argued Cantrell wanted to stop Rosa from testifying to a grand jury about corruption in the police department.

With the help of Wyoming superlawyer Gerry Spence, Cantrell was acquitted. He took work as a range detective in South Dakota and later moved back to Rock Springs.

In 2004, Cantrell died in a Salt Lake City hospital at age seventy-six and was buried in Rock Springs. A feature film about Cantrell's life, *Quick Draw: A True Story,* is said to be in the works.

Michael Rosa (1949–1978) was buried in his native New York. See also Outlaw/Lawman Tom Horn (Cheyenne).

CHINESE MASSACRE
Rock Springs

The historic Chinatown covered several square blocks north of the downtown area surrounding what is now Bridger Avenue. A monument to the tragedy is planned at the southwest corner of Bridger Avenue and M Street, the heart of the district (GPS 41.59119, -109.21883).

In 1885, racial tensions simmered in Rock Springs because Chinese coal miners were paid less than their white counterparts, causing many white workers to be skipped over in favor of cheaper Chinese labor. Worse, the Rock Springs hostilities were part of a bigger anti-Chinese sentiment all over the American West at the time.

On September 2, the conflict boiled over. A gang of white men attacked Chinese workers at one coal mine, and the riot spread like wildfire. By afternoon, two armed and angry white mobs had invaded Chinatown, shooting at men, women, and children, plundering homes, and setting fire to buildings.

By nightfall, seventy-five homes were destroyed and twenty-eight Chinese were dead. Survivors fled to nearby towns until they were escorted back to Rock Springs by federal troops a few days later. They found only scorched earth and the decomposing, badly burned bodies of loved ones being eaten by wild animals.

Sixteen men were arrested for their roles in the massacre, but a grand jury refused to indict them. Upon leaving the jail, the men were met by rousing applause from local citizens. Nobody was ever prosecuted in the massacre.

Some past archaeological work was done in the heart of Chinatown in the vacant lot across from St. Cyril's Catholic Church, 633 Bridger Ave. (GPS 41.591478, -109.219438).

A few local history exhibits explore the massacre today. The Rock Springs Historical Museum at 201 B St. (GPS 41.58527, -109.22082) has some material. The Sweetwater County Museum in Green River, 3 East Flaming Gorge Way in Green River Springs' Chinatown, includes tapestries, ceremonial pewter items, gongs, and clothing.

FRONTIER SERIAL KILLER'S GRAVE?
South Pass City

South Pass City State Historic Site is two miles off WY 28, thirty-eight miles south of Lander, Wyoming. It is only open May 15–September 30, daily 9–6; www.southpasscity.com. The Boot Hill Cemetery is a quarter mile south of the site on South Pass City Road, at GPS 42.46390, -108.80277.

A strange thing was happening in Polly Bartlett's inn near the gold-rush town of South Pass City: Rich travelers were dying all too frequently. More than a dozen travelers—most carrying gold—fell dead at the inn, presumably poisoned.

When the marshal began to suspect foul play—or so the local legend says—Polly fled, but she was captured near Jackson Hole and returned to South Pass for trial. By now, Polly was known as the "Murderess of Slaughterhouse Gulch."

Angry locals didn't wait for a judge to pass sentence. One night in the late 1860s or early 1870s, a vigilante broke into the South Pass City jail and literally cut Polly in half with a shotgun blast as she stood in the calaboose's day room area. The jail still exists at GPS 42.467858, -108.801877.

Polly Bartlett's inn is said to have been somewhere in Slaughterhouse Gulch at GPS 42.37884, -108.72011.

Polly and her victims were reportedly buried in the town's Boot Hill cemetery, but their markers were all made of wood—if their graves were marked at all. Today, because of time and weather, their grave locations have been lost.

THE CRIME BUFF'S GUIDE TO THE OUTLAW ROCKIES

This restored mining camp includes twenty original structures from the local livery stable and school to saloons and homes. Legend also says Butch Cassidy used to stand in the door of the Miner's Exchange Saloon (GPS 42.46821, -108.801223) and flip stolen silver dollars to kids in the dusty street. You might even hear a few stories about Calamity Jane's exploits in South Pass—but like the town itself, original documentation is hard to come by. Like so much of the West's history, myth must sometimes suffice.

SPRING CREEK RAID
Tensleep area

A historical marker exists at the site about six miles southeast of Tensleep on WY 434 at GPS 43.95543, -107.38819.

Real-life conflicts between cattlemen and sheep growers in Wyoming provided many Hollywood plots, but for the people involved, they were deadly.

The last of the armed skirmishes between the foes happened at the Allemand Ranch on Spring Creek in Wyoming's Nowood Valley on April 2, 1909.

Late that night, anti-sheep raiders attacked the sheep camp of Joe Allemand and four herders, setting fire to their wagons. Two herders escaped, but Allemand and two of his hands were killed.

Today two cairns mark the spots where the sheep wagons were parked. The south wagon was at GPS 43.955539, -107.387769 and the north wagon at GPS 43.95790, 7-107.388799.

Seven men were eventually arrested. Two testified against the others at a trial in Basin, Wyoming. As a result three were convicted of murder and the other two of arson. The killers spent less than five years in prison.

The dead sheepmen were buried side by side near the creek behind the Allemand ranch house. Those graves are on private property, and access is not allowed. Surviving herder **Bounce**

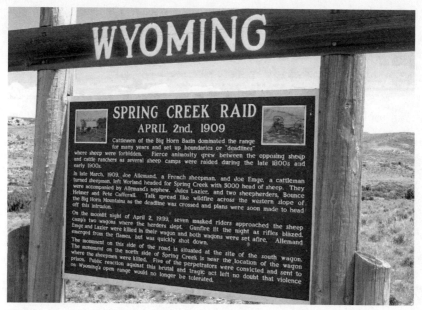

The cairn behind this roadside sign marks one of two nearby spots where the last major crime in Wyoming's range wars happened.

Helmer, then a teenager, lived in the area the rest of his life. Helmer (1890–1956) is buried in the Tensleep Cemetery in Lot 3, or GPS 44.03724, -107.45174. Two of the convicted raiders are also buried in Tensleep: **Ed Eaton** (1856–1912) died from a tick bite in prison and is buried at GPS 44.03694, -10745252, and **Milton Alexander** (1861–1931) is at GPS 44.03692, -107.45226.

The Pioneer Museum, 500 South 2nd St. in Tensleep (GPS 44.03399, -107.44504), has some interpretive displays about the crime. The Wyoming State History Museum, 2301 Central Ave. in Cheyenne (GPS 41.139427, -104.818022) owns a judge's gavel that was made from the burned sheepwagons in the Spring Creek Raid.

The building where the killer cowboys' trial was held still exists in Basin. The former courthouse—now the Basin City Arts Center—is at 117 South 4th St., or GPS 44.380514, -108.038789.

WILEY FAMILY MASSACRE
Thermopolis

The Wiley family home was at 513 US 20 North, or GPS 43.701944, -108.179722. This is private property.

Everybody thought Jamie Wiley was a good kid. At fifteen, he was a clean-cut honor student, a churchgoer, a high school wrestler, a baritone horn player in the band, a lifeguard at a local pool, and a student council leader.

So it shocked the small town of Thermopolis when Jamie was named as the key suspect in the mass murder of his stepmother Becky and three siblings—Jesse, thirteen, Willy, ten, and Tyrone, five.

Police say Jamie argued with his stepmother after school on November 24, 1990, then killed her with a shotgun. He then shot Jesse and Tyrone, while Willy fled the house. But Jamie caught Willy in the front yard, dragged him back inside, and blew off his

Becky Wiley and three of her sons were buried in Buffalo after a 1990 massacre by her oldest son, Jamie, in Thermopolis.

head with a shotgun blast. Jamie then set the family's rural trailer ablaze and drove a mile to a neighbor's house to call firefighters.

In 1991, Jamie pleaded guilty to arson, three counts of second-degree murder, and one count of first-degree murder—because it required premeditation to chase down Willy, bring him back to the house, and kill him. He was sentenced to life in prison, where he remains today.

Becky Wiley (1956–1990) and three of her sons were buried together in Buffalo's Willow Grove Cemetery, 351 North Adams Ave. The graves are in Block 85, Lot 16, or GPS 44.33123, -106.70461.

LITTLE JOSEPH TRIESCHMAN'S GRAVE
Mammoth Hot Springs, Yellowstone NP

Fort Yellowstone Army Cemetery is north of Mammoth Hot Springs, just west of US 89/North Entrance Rd., near the park's riding corrals. The grave is at GPS 44.96437, -110.70035.

Margaret Trieschman, wife of Fort Yellowstone's post carpenter and mother of four, was suicidal. In 1899, she tried to kill herself by slicing her own throat with a butcher knife but failed. As a result, she was sent to a Montana insane asylum for a few months, after which she was declared cured.

But a few days after she returned home to Fort Yellowstone, she proved them all wrong. She snatched her five-year-old son Joseph and hacked off his head with a knife while his three siblings watched. Margaret, still wielding the bloody knife, then chased the other children to a neighbor's house, where she was subdued.

A prosecutor soon declared Margaret to be insane and ordered that she be taken by train to a government asylum in Washington, D.C. But Margaret surprised them again: She leaped from the train as it passed over a bridge that spanned the Yellowstone River in Montana, and her body was never found.

Little Joseph was buried in the Army cemetery beneath an elaborate headstone. His siblings grew up and were influential in park activities; his brother Harry became a prominent ranger for whom the park's Trieschman Knob (GPS 44.339444, -110.8775) is named.

Five-year-old Joseph Trieschman was beheaded by his insane mother in one of Yellowstone's darkest moments.

ACKNOWLEDGMENTS

A book such as this requires a passionate, unofficial, and unpaid support staff to point the way to the places I've described. As always, chief among them is my devoted wife, Mary, who has ridden shotgun on most of my ghost-chasing explorations. She spent thirty-five days and 8,300 miles with me on this book, and remains married to me. When a man drags his wife to dozens of muddy cemeteries, old crime scenes, and presumably haunted buildings, and she tells him she wouldn't want to be anywhere else, then he knows he chose the right one.

One special day in my research stands out. Archaeologist David Darlington supplied the four-wheelers, beer, and antelope sausage for a day in the remote outlaw hangout of Powder Wash, Wyoming. It was not a trip back in time but a trip into a place forgotten entirely by time. Magical.

Other people were also important in some small but important ways, earning my respect and gratitude. So many thanks are owed to editor Erin Turner at Globe Pequot, my agent Gina Panettieri, Johan P. Bakker, Patrick Brower, Dan Brumbaugh, Rita Butler, Amy Cashel, Beryl Churchill, Charles and Leslie Clapper, Laurena Mayne Davis, Geoff Dobson, Dave Dovala, Craig Douglass and Catherine Richard, Bob Edwards, Rick Ewig, Sharon Field, Dr. George Gill, Earl and Kathy Gipe, Frank and Jackie Graham, Terrick and Alyssa Hagen, Dan Haley, Steve Henson, Bernie and Adria Hohman, Linda Holloway, Conrad Hopp Jr., Grayce Keller, Danette Kinsley, Rod Laird, Earl and Barbara Madsen, Mary McKinstry of the Fort Sedgwick Historical Society, Kirk Mitchell, Jessica Monday, Bill and Susan Pennington, Julie and Dan Perala, Dr. Phil Roberts, Stone Saville, Lynn Smith, Starcraft RV Inc., Guy and Bonnie Thompson, Thomas Trotman, Kevin Vaughan, Rod Warne, Pat Watson, James Wetzel, Wyoming State Archives, and all those who often knew literally where the bodies were buried.

ACKNOWLEDGMENTS

To my fellow authors Larry Brown, Dan Buck, Anne Meadows, Chip Carlson, Frank J. Daniels, Debra Faulkner, Robert Hardaway, Steve Jackson, Dick Kreck, Rick Mattix, Carol McNew, Dr. Jerred Metz, Victoria Newman, Silvia Pettem, and Kevin Sullivan, who all offered expert reflection.

And to all the rest who happily led me through their homes, scribbled directions, said "follow me," called other people "who should know," and shared memories that nobody ever asks about anymore.

Ron Franscell
San Antonio, Texas

INDEX

Italicized page numbers indicate
  photographs.

A

Abshier, George, 50–51, 68–70
actors and actresses, 79–80, 116
Aguilar, Frank, 48–49
Ainslie, Bob, 173, 174
airplane bombings, 10–12, *11*
Alcorn, Sankey and Gordon, 22
Alexander, Milton, 219
Allemand, Joe, 218
Allison, Clay, 70–71
Alterie, Jack, 105–6, *106*
Ammons, Elias, 88
Andrade, Allen, 65
Angus, William "Red," 146, 148
Argento, Arthur, 203, 205
Arridy, Joe, 48–49
Averill, Jim, 157–59

B

Baker, D. M., 202, 204
Banker, Jaylene, 214
bank robberies, 7–9, 23–25, 32, 50–51,
  68–70, 99–100, 114–15, 119, 121, 127, 137,
  203
Barber, Amos, 146, 147, 163, 170
Barker, Herman, 201
Barker, Lloyd, 41–42
Bartlett, Polly, 217
Bassett, Ann, 130–32, *131*
Bassett, Josie, 130, *131*, 131–32
Bates, John D., 25–26
Bechtel, Amy Wroe, 156, 184–86
Belle of the West saloon, 189–90
Bender, Dick, 132
Beni, Jules, 90
Benson, Kelley and Linda, 109–10
Berg, Alan, 6
Bernall, Cassie, 35, 66–67
Berrelez, Aleszandra, 3–4
Best, Jim, 212
Billy the Kid, 115
Biscaro, Al, 212
Blachley, Andrew, 99
Black Kettle, 81–82
Blagg family murders, 108–9, *109*
Blonger, Lou, 27
Boettcher, Charles, II, 21–22, 30, 31
bombings, 10–12, *11*, 171–72, *172*, 177–78
bondsmen, 56

Bonney, William H., 115
Booth, Bill, 151
bounty hunters, 23
Breeden, Spicer, 65–66
Bridges, Jim, 178
brothels and bordellos, *28*, 28–29, 152,
  192, 192–94
Brown, Bobby, 56
Brown, Carlene, 214
Brown, Cleveland, Jr., 212, *213*
Browne, Robert Charles, 56–57
Brown Palace murders, 14–15, *15*
Browns Park, 130
Bryant, Kobe, 100–101
Buffalo Bill Historical Center, 170–71
bulldozer rampages, 106–8, *107*, 178–79
Bundy, Ted, 92, 94–96, *95*
Burke, Dell, *192*, 194
Burns, Lester, 117
Burridge, Amy, 153–54
Bush family murders, 117–18, *118*
bus stop murders, 13
Byung, Park Hee, 32

C

Calamity Jane, 191, 218
Callahan, Henry, 46–47
Campbell, Caryn, 92, 94
cannibals, 29, 31, 51, 110–14, *111*, *112*
Canton, Frank, 145, 146, 148, 151–52
Cantrell, Ed, 214–16, *215*
Carlino, Pete, 39
Carlino, Sam, 39
Carlisle, Bill, 188–89
Carroll, Paul, 211
Carver, Will, 121, 140
Cassidy, Butch, 119–35, *122*, 137, 138–39, 218
cattlemen wars, 145–49, *146*, *147*, 156–59,
  218–19, *219*
Champion, Nate, 145–46, *146*, 146–47, 149
Chapel Hill Memorial Gardens, 3–5
Chapman, Duane "Dog," 23, 56
Chase, John B., 87, 88
Chatterton, Fenimore, 164
Cheesman Park, 17–19, 37, 130
Chinese massacre, 216–17
Chivington, John, *81*, 81–83, 84
Chuck E. Cheese murders, 1
Church, Heather Dawn, 56
Church, John and Louella, 200–201
church massacres, 54–55, *55*
cliff falls, 181–82, *182*

Clifton, Diamond L. Slim, 200–201
clones, 179–80
Coble, John, 163, 164
Cody, William F. "Buffalo Bill," 72–73, *73*, 90
Cokeville Elementary School bombing, 171–72, *172*
Collins, Arthur L., 30
Collison, Merle, 173, 174
Colorado Historical Society, 30–31
Columbia Cemetery, 46
Columbine High School massacre, 5, 33, 35, 66–67
Cook, David J., 32
Cooley, Melanie, 92, 95
Coors, Adolph, III, 37, 74–76
Corbett, Joe, 37, *74*, 74–76, *75*
Cornett, Don, 143–44
coroners, 143–44
Cox, Tipton, 203, 205
Cunningham, Julie, 92, 95
Curry, George "Flat Nose," 136, 140

D

Dale, Virginia, *89*, 89–91
Davis, "Dangerous Dick," 193
decapitations, 179–80, *180*, 221–22, *222*
Denver Mint robbery, 7–9, *8*, 32
DePooter, Corey, 5, 35
Dia, Oumar, 13
dissections, 207–8
doctors, 191–92, 207–9
Dodson, Janice and John Bruce, 97–98
dogs, 5, *5*
Douglas Cemetery, 175
Duke family murders, 181–82, *182*
Dunlap, Nathan, 1
Durand, Earl, *202*, 202–5, *204*
Dyer, Elias Foster, 52

E

Eaton, Dale Wayne, 155–56, 185–86
Eaton, Ed, 219
Ehlers, Lisa, 144–45
Elder, Cher, 59–60
Enderlin, Elizabeth Spurgeon, 47
Enron, 119
Espinosa brothers, 63–64
Evans, John, 30, 83
executions, 1, 3, 48–51, 49–50, 151–52, 164, 174, 178, 184, 211–13, *213*

F

Faber, Charlie, 70–71
Fairmount Cemetery, 27–30
Fall, Albert B., 199–200

Farmers and Merchants Bank robbery, 99–100, *100*
fathers, murders of, 165–67, *166*
filmmakers, 168
First National Bank robbery, 50–51, 68–70, *69*
Fleagle Gang, 50–51, 68–70, *69*
Fleming, Kelly, 35, 36–37
football players, 16–17
Ford, Robert, *57*, 57–59
forensic geology, 97–98
Freeze, John, 50
Fremont Canyon Bridge murder, 152–55, *153*
Fugate, Caril, 173–74

G

game wardens, 196–98, *197*
gangsters, 27, 37–39, *39*, 41–42, 80, 105–6, 201
Garrison, Sylvester Lee, 1, 3
Gawthrop, Johnny, 203, 205
Gimlin, Frank, 212
Glava, Fodor, 67–68
Golden Cemetery, 65–67
Gonzales, Annaletia Marie, 16
Goodell, Henry, 116
Gordon, Michael, Jr., 79–80
Graham, Jack, 10–12, *11*, 29
Green, Jeffrey, 177–78
Greene, Linda, *168*, 168–69
Griffith, Emily, 30, 76–79, *77*, *78*
Griffith, Florence, 30, 77, *77*
Gross, Christy, 214
Gurtner, Ethel and Evans, 78–79

H

Haggard, Ted, 54–55
Hahn, Anna Marie, 52–54
Hahn, Philip, 52
Harkins, Henry, 64
Harrington, Orville, *8*, 8–9
hate crimes, 64–65, 186–88, *187*. See also racism
Hawkins, Aubrey, 91
Hazen, Josiah, 135, 175
Heath, Lillian, 208, 209
Heemeyer, Marvin, 106–8, *107*
Heflin, Earl, 173–74
Helmer, Bounce, 219–20
Henderson, Russell, 186–88, *187*
Henry, Aggie Watkins, 116
Henwood, Frank, 14–15
Hickok, Wild Bill, 191
Highlands Ranch, 15
Hinman, Gary Allen, 104–5
hit-and-run victims, 65–66

Hole-in-the-Wall, 121, 128–29
Holliday, John Henry "Doc," 88–89, 101–4, *102, 103*
Hoofprints of the Past Museum, 149
Hopkinson, Mark, 177–78
Horn, Tom, 46, 99, 110, 145, 160–65, *161, 162,* 210
Hotel Colorado, 105
Howard, Dorothy Gay, 44–46, *45*
Howe, Sam, 31
Humphrey, Jack and Rita, 176–77
hunting trip murders, 97–98
husband killers, 19–21, *20*

I
insider trading scandals, 25
Irvine, William, 146, 147
Ives, Edward, 50

J
Jaehnig, Matthaeus, 66
Jahnke family murders, *166,* 166–67
jails, 125–26, *126,* 191
James, Jesse, murderer of, *57,* 57–59
Jane Does, 44–46, *45*
Jenkins, Jerry, 154
Jim Gatchell Museum, 148
Johnson County War, 145–49, *146, 147,* 152, 158
judges, 52, 169–70
Julien, James P., gallow inventions of, 164–65, 210, 212

K
Kechter, Matthew, 35, 37
Kennedy, Ron, 154–55
Kesinger, Everett, 68, 70
Ketchum, Sam, 121, 140
Ketchum, Tom, 140
kidnappings, 3–5, *5,* 21–22, 37, 74–76, *75,* 153–55
Kilpatrick, Ben, 121, 140
Kimball, Scott Lee, 39
Kimmell, Lisa Marie, 155–56
King, Daisy, 10–12, 29
King, James W., 23–25, *24*
King, Stephen, 61–62
Kirkham, Jane, 71
Kohler, Ernst, 53
Korean freedom fighters, 32

L
Lacey, John W., 163
Lakanen, Bill, 196–98, *197*
Lakeview Cemetery, 169–70
Lamont, Hobert W., 26

Lane, David, 63
Laska, Ben, 31
Law, George, 114–15, *115*
law enforcement museums, 210–11
law enforcement officer memorials, 3, *4,* 175–76
law enforcement officers, 25–27, 32, 50, 59, 66, 70–71, 88–89, 101–4, 110, 159, 165, 175, 214–16
Lay, Elzy, 121, 123, 137, 140
Lay, Kenneth, 119
LeFors, Joe, 163, 165
Lewis, Chuck, 202, 204
Lil Miss murder, 155–56
Linaberry, Orville, 203, 205
Linderfelt, Karl, 87, 88
Locke, J. G., 28
Logan, Harvey "Kid Curry," 104, 121, 135, *136,* 136–37, *137,* 175
Londoner, Wolfe, 29
Long, Royal Russell, 214
Longet, Claudine, 96–97
Lopez, Greg, 65–66
Ludlow massacre, 85–88, *86*
Lundgren, Edward, 68
Lundy, Fred, 77–78
Luther, Tom, 59–60
lynchings, 156–59, 190, 200–201, 207

M
madams, *28,* 28–29, 47, 152, 193–95
Maghee, Thomas, 208
Malten, John, 196–98, *197*
Mankoff, Phillip, 25
Manson family murders, 104–5
Maple, Dale, 31
masks, death, *206,* 208
Masterson, Bat, 59, 88–89, 102
Mauser, Daniel, 35, 36
McAuliffe, Cindy and Debby, 182–84, *183*
McCall, Jack, 191
McCarty brothers, 99–100, *100,* 127, 132, 138
McCormick, Michael and Tom, 84–85
McGovern, Edward P., 18–19, 37
McKinney, Aaron, 186–88, *187*
McLeod, Kaysi Dawn, 39
McParland, James, 35–36
Medicine Bow General Store, 195, *195*
Meeker Bank robbery, 114–15, *115*
Meeker Hotel, 115
Meeks, Henry Wilbur "Bob," 137–38
Meldrum, Bob, 98
Mercer, Asa, 148
Meyer, Debra, 214
miners, 30, 85–88, *87*

Miner's Exchange Saloon, *133*, 133–34, 218
Monge, Luis, 49–50
Moore, Ace, 189–90
Morris, Esther Hobart, 169–70
Mother Featherlegs, 193
mountain men, *202*, 202–5, *204*
Mount Olivet Cemetery, 36–37
Munis, David and Robin, 167
Murray, Matthew, 54–55, *55*
Museum of Colorado Prisons, 51

N
Nacchio, Joe, 25
Nemnich, Jerry, 110
Nettie's Place, 152
Newberry, Donald, 91
New Life Church massacre, 54–55, *55*
Nickell, Willie and Kels, 161–63, 170

O
Obendoerfer, Johan, 53
Occidental Hotel, 149–51, *150*
O'Day, Tom, 140
Ohnhaus, Charles, 165
O'Kelley, Ed, 58–59
Old Trail Town and Museum of the Old
    West, 129, *129*
Oliverson, Denise, 92, 95
Orahood, Harper, 84
Order, The, 6
Osborn, Arthur, 201
Osborne, John, 208–9
Outlaw Cave, 128
outlaws, Old West, 70–71, 89–91, 98,
    99–100, 135, 151–52, 156–59, 170–71,
    174–75, 189–90. *See also* Cassidy, Butch;
    Horn, Tom; Sundance Kid; Wild Bunch

P
Pacheco, John and Louis, 50
Packer, Alfred, 29, 31, 51, 110–14, *111*, *112*
Parks, Hermie, 117
Parrish, John and A. N., 68, 69–70
Parrott, George "Big Nose," 205–9, *206*, *207*
Patterson, Charles and Gertrude Gibson,
    19–21
Phul, Tony von, 14–15
Pierce, "Kid," 114–15, *115*
Pike, George, 175
Pinkerton agents, 35–36
Pixley, Andrew, 182–84, *183*
Place, Etta, 123, 124, 140
police officers. *See* law enforcement entries
political corruption, 198–200, *199*
Porter, Fanny, 124, 141
Powder Wash hideout, 132–33

Powell, Mack, 88
prison cemeteries, 48–51, *49*, 211–13, *213*
prisons, 51, 62–63, 91, 127, 209–11, *210*.
    See also jails
prostitutes, *28*, 38–39, 47, 152, 193–95
Pry, Polly, 29

R
racism, 6, 13, 28, 216–17
Ramsey, JonBenét, 42–44, *43*
rapists, 16, 60, 100–101, 110, 153–55,
    182–84, 191–92
Ray, Nick, 145, 146–47
Rice, Laura Lee, and children, 179–80, *180*
Richards, William A., 127, 170
Richthofen Castle, 19–21, *20*
Ricker, Charles, 159
Riley, James "Doc" Middleton, 174–75
Rivas, George, 91
Riverside Cemetery, 31–32
Robertson, Shelley, 92, 95
Rockefeller, John D., Jr., 86, 88
rodeo murders, 213–14
Rohrbaugh, Daniel, 35
roller-skating brothels, 152
Roma, Joseph, 39
Romer, Bill, 173, 174
Roosevelt, Buddy, 116
Rosa, Michael, 214, 216
Ross, Allen, *168*, 168–69
Royston, Howard, 51, 68–70
Ruhl, Henry, 211

S
Sabich, Vladimir "Spider," 96–97
Sable Lake, 117
saloons, *133*, 133–34, 189–90, 196, 218
Samaritan Foundation, 168
Samson (bull elk), 60–61, *61*
Sand Creek Massacre, 32, 80–84, *81*, *82*, *83*
Sanders, Dave, 5, 35
Sanderson, Kenneth Standhope, 116
San Miguel Valley Bank robbery, 119, 127
San Vicente Cemetery, 139
Sarafin, Donnie, 143–44
school bombings, 171–72, *172*
school massacres, 5, 33, 35, 66–67
Scott, Rachel, 5, 35
serial killers, 16, 39, 52–54, 56–57, 63–64,
    84–85, 109–10, 217–18
Shepard, Matthew, 186–88, *187*
Shining, The (King), 61–62
Shirley, Jim, 114–15, *115*
Shoels, Isaiah, 29
shoes, human skin, *206*, 208
Shores, Cyrus Wells, 110

Short, Elizabeth "Black Dahlia," 79–80
Silks, Mattie, *28,* 28–29
Simpson, Don, 196–98, *197*
Sisty, Wilson E., 32
Skinner's Bar, 134
Slade, Jack, *89,* 89–91
Smaldone brothers, 37–39, *38*
Smith, Soapy, 59
Snyder, William, 88
soap kettle murders, 117–18, *118*
socialites, 14–15, *15*
Soule, Silas, 30, 82, *83,* 84
South Pass City, 217–18
Spinuzzi, Joseph "Scotty," 80
Spring Creek Campground, 188–89
Spring Creek Raid, 158, 218–19, *219*
Springer, Isabel and John W., 14–15, *15*
stagecoach robberies, 71
Stanley Hotel, 61–62
Starkweather, Charlie, 173–74
Story, John, 191–92
Strouss, Emil W., 19–21
Sun, Tom, 158
Sundance Kid, 120–35, *122, 126,* 139
Supermax Prison, 62–63
Sweetwater Ranch, 105

T
talk-radio hosts, 6
TA Ranch, 146, 148
Taylor, Talton, 211
teachers, 30, 76–79, *77, 78*
Teapot Rock, 198–200, *199*
Texas Seven, 91
Thill, Nathan, 13
Thompson, John D., 179
Thomson, Becky, 153–54
Tikas, Louis, 87, 88
Tisdale, John A., 147, *147*
Tobin, Tom, 64
Tomlin, John, 35
Townsend, Lauren, 35
Tracy, Harry, 98, 132, 140
Trainor, Nick, 7, 32
train robberies, 122, 123, 134–35, 188–89, 206
transgender murders, 64–65
treason convictions, 31
Trieschman, Joseph, 221–22, *222*
Turpin, Victoria Lyn, 16

U
union disputes, 30, *85,* 85–88
United Bank robbery, 23–25, *24*
United Flight 629, 10–12, *11*

V
vampires, 67–68, 168
Van Cise, Philip, 27
Vanderjagt, Bruce, 66
VanVelkinburg, Jeannie, 13, 39
Vehar, Vincent, 177–78
Vincents, Henry H., 176, 209
Virginia Dale Station, *89,* 89–91
Virginian, The (Wister), 150, 194–95
Virginian Hotel, 196

W
Warner, Matt, 127, 132, 141
Watson, Ella "Cattle Kate," 156–59
Wesson, Gil, 116
White, Byron Raymond, 9
White, Richard Paul, 16
Widdowfield, Robert, 176, *207,* 209
Wieghard, Robert, 47
wife killers, 167
Wild Bunch, 98, 114–15, *115,* 119–41, *122, 126, 131, 133, 137,* 165, 175
Wiley family massacre, *220,* 220–21
Williams, Cy, 190
Williams, Darrent, 16–17
Willoughby, Troy Dean, 144–45
Winstanley, Arthur, 26–27
Wister, Owen, 149–50, 194–96, *195*
Wolcott, Frank, 146, 148
Woodard, Charlie, 159
Woodpecker Hill Prison Cemetery, 48–51, *49*
Works, Rachel and Stephanie, 54
Wright, Nettie, 152
writers, 149–50, 194–96, *195*
Wyoming Frontier Prison Museum, 209–11, *210*
Wyoming Law Enforcement Academy, 175–76
Wyoming Peace Officers Memorial, 175–76, 198
Wyoming Peace Officers Museum, 210–11
Wyoming State Penitentiary Cemetery, 211–13, *213*
Wyoming Territorial Prison Park, 127

Y
Yellow Hotel, *192,* 194
Yogi (bloodhound), 4–5, *5*
Young, David and Doris, 171–72, *172*

Z
Zapata, Justin "Angie," 64–65

ABOUT THE AUTHOR

Ron Franscell is a bestselling author and journalist whose atmospheric true crime/memoir *The Darkest Night* was hailed as a direct descendant of Truman Capote's *In Cold Blood* and established him as one of the most provocative new voices in narrative nonfiction. His work as appeared in the *Washington Post, Chicago Sun-Times, San Francisco Chronicle, Denver Post, San Jose Mercury-News, St. Louis Post-Dispatch,* and *Milwaukee Journal-Sentinel. The Crime Buff's Guide to the Outlaw Rockies* is his fifth book. His other Globe Pequot Press titles are *The Crime Buff's Guide to Outlaw Texas* and *The Sourtoe Cocktail Club.* Ron grew up in Wyoming and now lives in Texas.

PHOTO BY MARY FRANSCELL